AWAKENING YOUR "DEAD ZONE"

For all too many American women, the pelvic region represents a sensual "dead zone". But in many other cultures, this part of the body is the focus of special training that enables a woman to both obtain and give the ultimate in sexual pleasure.

This definitive book offers such training, explores the most up-to-date scientific information about female sexuality, and provides a uniquely personal program for enhancing sexual pleasure.

THE LOVE MUSCLE

About the author:

BRYCE BRITTON is one of America's premier sex therapists. She has a masters degree in psychology and is a founder of Eve's Garden, the feminist sexuality organization.

SIGNET and MENTOR Books of Interest

THE LOVE MUSCLE

EVERY WOMAN'S GUIDE TO INTENSIFYING SEXUAL PLEASURE

by Bryce Britton

with Belinda Dumont

Illustrated by Bonnie Hofkin

A SIGNET BOOK

NEW AMERICAN LIBRARY

TIMES MIRROR

SIGNET TRADEMARK REG. U.S. PAT. OFF. AND FOREIGN COUNTRIES
REGISTERED TRADEMARK—MARCA REGISTRADA
HECHO EN CHICAGO, U.S.A.

SIGNET, SIGNET CLASSIC, MENTOR, PLUME, MERIDIAN and NAL BOOKS
are published by The New American Library, Inc.,
1633 Broadway, New York, New York 10019

First Signet Printing, October, 1983

1 2 3 4 5 6 7 8 9

PRINTED IN THE UNITED STATES OF AMERICA

This book is dedicated to my families—the Minors, the Morrises, and my family of friends.

—*Bryce Britton*

To Joseph S. Lombardi, from Joe-knows-who, for Joe-knows-why.

—*Belinda Dumont*

The help and unselfish cooperation of many individuals have made *The Love Muscle* unique. I could not have done this book alone. I would particularly like to thank the following people: Catherine Bryce, Andrea Sertucha, Fred Weaver III, Whitney Young, Sam Anderson, Hope Cain, Gloria Gaev, David Lunney, Sandra Forrest, Donald Wright, Lonnie Barbach, Roger Libby, Dell Williams, Frania Zinns, Betty Kan, Nicholas Charney, Wayne and Jackie McGloughlin, Laurie Young, Marian Hunter, Bill Blair, Belinda Dumont, Richard and Patricia Peacock, and Jill Neimark.

I acknowledge all of the women who supported my workshops and practice. It's their courage, honesty, trust, and integrity that made *The Love Muscle* a reality.

—*Bryce Britton*

For their unfailing help and backing I want to thank my mom and dad, Charles and Augusta Citron, and my son, Patrick. I would also like to acknowledge Dr. Alex Comfort, who affected me as I believe he affects all those whose lives he touches. To physiologist and coach John Gregor Garb, formerly of the Santa Clara Swim Club, my eternal respect and thanks. Thank you also to Dale and Joel Berson, their children, Erika and Jeremy, and to Roberta and Joel Tilem and their three sons, Peter, Andrew, and Matthew, good and dear friends all, without whom I could not have done this book.

—*Belinda Dumont*

Contents

Introduction   1

Chapter 1
The Love Muscle: Prescription for Pleasure   6

Chapter 2
Preparation for Orgasm   42

Chapter 3
Making the Mind-Body Connection   73

Chapter 4
Creating and Controlling Orgasm   99

Chapter 5
Intimacy: The Excitement of Sharing with a
Partner   156

Chapter 6
Exercises and Sexual Aids for the Advanced   210

Chapter 7
Sex, Health, and Fitness   242

Introduction

When I was going to college in San Diego, a good friend of mine was drafted and sent to Vietnam. Naturally, we continued our friendship through letters. There's one in particular I'll never forget. *That* letter is one of the reasons for this book. In it my friend told of his first visit to a whorehouse (controlled by the U.S. military). It shocked me. He said that the Vietnamese women he had sex with held his penis inside them in a viselike grip, yet they could loosen up and feel like silk when they wanted to. He said they could milk him to orgasm, hardly moving their hips at all. He asked why sex had been so different with women in California.

As I read his letter my heart pounded and I was filled with intense curiosity. What did these women know that I didn't? More than that, how could I learn to do such things?

It wasn't until years later that I found out what my friend had meant. Like so many other women, when I learned about sex I certainly didn't realize it had anything to do with controlling my inner muscles. All that came later, when I chose to make my career in sex therapy and education. Up until that time, I had decided that special sexual knowledge was a myth.

After I trained as a sexual therapist, I became aware that other cultures *do* teach their women to give and get sexual pleasure, as a matter of course, by training their sexual muscles. As a feminist I wondered whether this was just another skill oriented toward pleasing the male. Then I discovered that interior exercise is the foundation method for achieving orgasm and greatly increasing a female's sexual pleasure, as well as being vital for her health.

When I started giving workshops in sexual enhancement, I began to hear women share their sexual insecurities and fears. As I conducted more workshops I became aware that the main concern of women was their lack of control over whether they reached orgasm, and the stress that lack of control caused them. Women reported several types of orgasm, as did I. Maybe the popular sex manuals did encourage many women to attend the workshops. However, the stereotypic model of orgasm presented in these books often denied most of the women's personal experience, including my own.

The scientific research available at that time led mostly to pelvic exercises designed by a surgeon, Dr. Arnold Kegel. He prescribed them specifically for women suffering from urinary stress incontinence, a common malady that affects two-thirds of American women (his exercises are still the best treatment). He found that these exercises had surprising side effects— women who had never felt an orgasm before now did. Other women told the astonished Dr. Kegel that sex was never so great—they were having more orgasms and feeling them as never before!

Kegel's reports were published in obscure journals and never reached a wide public. Now, however, sexologists and therapists are close on the trail of the truth of sexual response. They are working with and testing the methods and conclusions of the pioneer sex researchers, Masters and Johnson. This research has begun to reveal new, totally unsuspected areas of sensitivity inside the vagina and uterus. Evidence is rapidly piling up that a woman can learn to control and experience a wide variety of orgasms. This research also applies to men. They can become multi-orgasmic by learning certain facts and doing a simple and pleasurable exercise program.

As soon as I discovered this research, I integrated pelvic exercises into my treatment programs and workshops. It has been the single most rewarding thing I have ever done. Many women tell me that these exercises have significantly increased their awareness of themselves and given them added sexual pleasure.

As important as enjoying sex more fully, or making your partner happier, is knowing that these exercises can alleviate a myriad of common sexual conditions that usually take people to the doctor. For example, regular love muscle exercise can help prevent hysterectomies and make for easier childbirth and quicker postpartum recovery. These same exercises can help parents educate their children who wet their beds. They also help old people by preventing senile vaginitis (aging of the vaginal walls from lack of lubrication) and the need for hormone replacement therapy. The information in this book is for everyone, and can make a happier, healthier you.

I am going to explore all the latest scientific information about sex, which will enable you to work out your own personal program of sexual enhancement. To do this, and make it fun, I use many

The pleasure of love

of the learning techniques and tension-reducing methods that will help you understand yourself and your sexuality and have been so successful with my workshop participants.

CHAPTER 1

The Love Muscle: Prescription for Pleasure

Her partner will then value her above all women, nor would he exchange her for the most beautiful Queen in the three worlds. So lovely and pleasant to the man is she who constricts.

Ananga Ranga, Sixteenth-century Indian sex text

The modern American woman might well ask, "Constricts what?" What is this mysterious element of sexuality, touted as the secret of sex itself, that Eastern and other cultures have taught their women? And, in more modern terms, what can it yield for the woman herself? Anything besides the male's enjoyment? The Indian teaching text I've cited goes on to say that this paragon of female sexuality must "ever strive to close and constrict the vagina until she holds the penis as with the fingers, opening and shutting at her pleasure, and finally acting as the hand of the milking girl, who milks the cow. This can only be learned by long practice, by throwing the will into the part affected." How can we learn to do that? And would we want to?

Well, the mysterious quality of the East is not mysterious. It is the workings of one of the major muscles of the human body: the *love muscle*, and modern science has now revealed its power to the woman who gains control of it. It is the means of creating and controlling orgasm. I am going to show you what it is, where it is, and how to use it, for your lifelong benefit and pleasure.

The Myth of the Myth

Are you wondering what I mean by this heading? Perhaps you're thinking to yourself, Masters and Johnson exposed the vaginal-versus-clitoral controversy as a myth, and the Hite Report backed them up. They both stated positively that orgasm comes from the clitoris.

Well, newly reported data show it ain't necessarily so. There's a vaginal side to orgasm, and it gives women more choice in experiencing sexual pleasure than ever before. I am going to make it available to you. These new data can be used to intensify orgasm through partner sex. That would be very good news— except for the *other* myth.

The other myth, and the whole trouble, started

with Freud, who said that women who had clitoral orgasms and not vaginal ones had immature feminine egos. This set us all up for the current clitoral-versus-vaginal controversy—that is, whether women achieve orgasm from stimulation of the clitoris or from thrusting of the penis in the vagina.

Most women who attended my sexuality workshops told me that none of these ideals or models really described their orgasm! The information available just did not fit their experience. The vaginal model created the myth of "normal orgasms." The clitoral model put pressure on both sexes and created a division between them. After these confusing times, we believe that the sexes can now be closer, both psychologically and physiologically, than ever before.

Until now, medical science had not resolved the controversy. I hope to end it here. There are many types of orgasm, and several ways to reach them. Orgasm is a continuum. That means that you can have an infinite variety of orgasms. Most important, your love muscle will help you to have them.

What Is The Love Muscle?

What is the love muscle? Its anatomical name is the *Pubococcygeus* muscle, or PC muscle for short. Although it is interwoven and surrounded by four sets of other pelvic muscles, it is the master muscle of the pelvis, slung like a hammock from front to back. When it is totally healthy and fit it is taut, held in a straight line. The love muscle spans a wider range than any other skeletal muscle, and unlike any other muscle, it can recover its function after years of disuse, sometimes in only a matter of weeks. It is also the muscle that contracts when you have an orgasm. Basically a sphincter muscle, it passes through the middle third of the vagina, forming a part of the urethra and the anus. Sphincter muscles are ring-shaped and surround entrances and passageways to the body.

For a long time, nobody thought too much about this muscle, except if it was involved in surgery. But two bold new discoveries have made us refocus our attention on this least-considered of body muscles and rethink the whole body of information on female sexuality.

Researchers have experimental evidence that there is more than one kind of woman's orgasm, and that women can actually ejaculate, despite the fact that they have no prostate gland. The latest research comes from John Perry and Beverly Whipple, a team from New Jersey, and Benjamin Graber, M.D., and Georgia Kline-Graber, at the University of Wisconsin. "We have films of the ejaculate squirting out in response to direct stimulation of an area called the Gräfenberg spot," Perry and Whipple report. The Gräfenberg spot is located in the anterior wall of the vagina, about an inch behind the pubic bone. "We think that spot is the female prostate," they report.

To find out if a woman was having an orgasm, Perry and Whipple didn't ask, but measured muscle tension in the vagina, particularly the forceful contractions of the PC muscle. But some women reported that they had had an orgasm, and a strong one, when the vaginal muscles showed little activity.

Other researchers have also recorded that some women experience orgasm deep in the uterus, *even when no clitoral stimulation is involved*.

Enter the love muscle.

In 1952 (a long time ago at the current rapid rate of advance in medical research), a Mayo Clinic-trained gynecologist and surgeon, Dr. Arnold Kegel, who taught at the University of Southern California, noticed a joyful, unexpected side effect of exercises he had developed for patients who had to undergo urinary surgery. These were PC muscle exercises, and they were so effective that he prescribed them not only after surgery but as an alternative to it, for gynecological or urinary problems. Kegel prescribed them because he repeatedly did surgery for certain conditions and six months later the woman would come back with the same problem. However, if they did the exercises that he prescribed, their conditions rapidly improved.

The side effect he didn't expect was that patients kept coming back and confiding that they were experiencing orgasm during intercourse for the first time, or more easily than ever before. The exercises seemed to give them more sensation in the vagina. Kegel reported his findings in prestigious journals, but the sexual side of his information never reached the public. In general, there was very little sexual information out before the public at all at that time.

Kegel's exercises were invented specifically for

women suffering from urinary stress incontinence. If you've ever had the unfortunate experience of wetting your pants while you were laughing or when carrying heavy groceries, you'll know what we mean. Especially after childbirth, urinary stress incontinence gets to be a problem for many women. It's been estimated that two-thirds of American women have this difficulty. The major cause of urinary stress incontinence is a weak love muscle. Kegel found the only effective way to alleviate this condition without surgery was to strengthen this muscle through physical exercise. His exercises are still the best remedy for this condition. If you suffer from urinary incontinence, this program will put a stop to it, *without surgery!* That is just one of the by-products of a healthy love muscle.

The message for you, however, is that healthy pelvic muscles, under *your* control, can give you all the ice cream flavors, all the rainbow colors of orgasm.

Most women are totally unaware of the crucial role their love muscle plays in their orgasm. Most of us now are familiar with the idea of fitness, if not actively involved in it. So the idea of exercising a specific muscle is no longer strange. At this point, I can sum up all the scientific research for you—*if you don't use it, you lose it*. As far as I'm concerned the evidence is conclusive: "An orgasm a day keeps the doctor away." A strong muscle, whether you wish to orgasm or just keep sexually fit, is your best insurance for your future happiness and good health.

About the Love Muscle

The love muscle is a major support muscle of your internal organs. It holds up all the organs of the abdomen and the pelvis. It's the muscle you were taught to control when you were toilet trained. It once controlled tail wagging! Because we walk upright these days, it takes excess strain, and can sag. For a woman, control leads to orgasm and good health. If a male trains and exercises this muscle, he will gain ejaculatory control and even have multiple orgasms. In chapter 5, on partnering, I will tell you more about this. I will show you exactly how to teach your lover how to locate his muscle, how and how much to exercise it, and how to use the love muscle with him to reach ecstasy in lovemaking. You will also learn some secrets of the male, and how to have penetration whether he is hard or not. In the vagina, your love muscle runs in a circular band with ringlike ridges, three-quarters of an inch to an inch wide. Later, I will guide you to feel these corrugations. The shape of the love muscle is different in different people, and it develops differently, too—although most women have a thicker muscle on the right side. During my training as a therapist, however, I found out that mine is thicker on the left. This reinforced my belief that each woman is anatomically different. It is important to acknowledge that your sexuality is unique, just as you are. Isn't it nice to know you're okay?

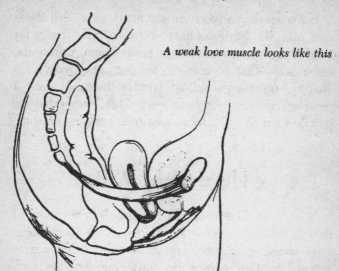

A weak love muscle looks like this

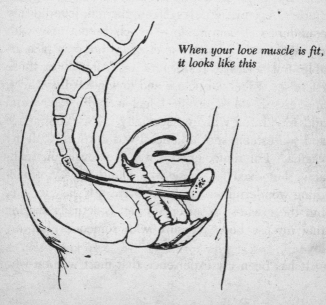

When your love muscle is fit, it looks like this

If we need an advertisement for orgasm, Bill Hartman and Marilyn Fithian, directors of the Center for Marital and Sexual Studies in Long Beach, California, did a study that concluded that orgasmic people are "happy, outgoing, well-adjusted individuals with a positive, optimistic attitude toward life." Nonorgasmic people tend to be "critical, negative, and pessimistic."

Orgasm at Will

What's it like to do love muscle exercises? I first introduced them at my sexuality workshops. One woman described them as "the life force in action." Another woman, previously nonorgasmic, said, "Orgasm blew the lid off my life." Other comments were, "As my muscles strengthened, so did my confidence. I communicate much better now with my sexual side." These exercises are not only pleasurable, but healthy. "It's beautiful." "After doing these exercises, I feel very close and loving toward others, and myself. Most of all, I feel incredibly powerful and integrated with my sexuality." "My confidence and self-esteem shot up once I was in touch with my vagina." For some, orgasm was previously unattainable, but even for those who found it easy, something wonderful was added. "Orgasm is easy for me, but the greatest experience of all is actually sharing that intense body pleasure with someone else, my love."

It has been my experience that most women who

can come with clitoral stimulation still want to come with a partner inside them. Dr. Hartman says, "Most married people do not masturbate regularly. I hear woman after woman tell me 'I want to come with my partner in me.'"

I want to give you the freedom to reach orgasm when *you* want to, with or without a partner. Wouldn't any woman want to be sure that she could have an orgasm at will? I think so.

You can capture control of your love muscle without destroying the intimacy of sex. Many people get nervous when they first try to identify their love muscle. It feels to them as if there's something wrong about approaching something so private clinically. Most people feel inhibited— that's only normal since exploring your sexuality is a profound experience. It can't take the spontaneity or chemistry out of sex. No matter what you know about yourself, the chemistry of attraction is a constant in the union between men and women. Rosemary Houghton, author of *Love* (Penguin) and a widely interviewed religious essayist, says, "Real love is effective. . . . If you really love you do something about it, and do it as well as you can manage to learn how."

My techniques have been developed to help you enhance your response. Then, once you master the secret of increasing your sexual pleasure, you have the option of sharing it with others.

Where Is Your Love Muscle?

To find your love muscle you'll be using a mental technique called creative visualization and a physical technique called isolation, borrowed from athletic theory. Most athletes learn how to "isolate" a muscle—in swimming, running, or dance, say—as a way to perfect a movement. Professionals learn how to focus their attention on one muscle at a time. As one of its functions, the muscle we're looking for now controls urine flow. It's the one you clench to cut off the flow. To make sure you have it in your mind, go to the bathroom and start to urinate. Then squeeze hard and stop the flow. Don't worry if you can't; just keep trying and you will succeed. Take your time; relax. Tighten again. That's your love muscle contracting. Concentrate on the sensation and you'll begin to memorize just how to contract it. It's amazing how quickly you can educate your mind to gain control over a muscle; like riding a bicycle, not rolling over onto your arch in running, or getting the backhand in tennis, only easier. By the time you've started and stopped the flow three times, you should have the feeling in your mind quite clearly. It is important to spread your legs, so the powerful buttock muscles don't interfere. What's critical is to feel how to squeeze your muscle. That pulled-up warm sensation is the key to sexual fitness. After you isolate the muscle, be sure to empty your bladder completely.

Many women are nervous about whether they can

identify their muscle. It's very normal *not* to be able to isolate this muscle when you first start out. Don't give up. Eventually the other exercises in this book will strengthen it so that it will be easy.

If you have isolated it, it feels good, doesn't it? After all, it's a new way of being in touch with yourself.

Are you backing away from the page at the mention of being in touch with yourself, pleasure, and orgasm? Please don't! If you're not already comfortable with the idea, I hope to help you become so. Pleasure is healthy. You will not turn into a sex maniac. You can gain from this information about keeping a healthy muscle, whether you want to use it for sexual pleasure or not. Barbara Walters once said, "I used to consider doing something just for pleasure a waste of time." But today women have a right to pleasure. Knowing pleasure from our bodies gives us power as people.

Getting to Know Me

The best fun we have at sexuality workshops is finding out what we really think about sex. In a way, once we come out into the open to share what we think and feel, *a lot of our ideas turn out to be just what everybody else believes!* After all, we all grew up with the same misinformation. Maybe we all learned it from the same neighborhood crowd! "Oh, ugh. Does he really put it in?" I can remember just not believing it. You can supply the rest of these yourself. Those old things die hard. We had to train *ourselves* in the art of love, with the help, at best, of loving partners. Really, there was no school where we could have learned it!

Most of us were taught that sex is something that happens spontaneously, that somehow you know how to do it. Despite all that the psychological/humanistic movement has taught us, it's hard to face the need for a little presex homework. But sex is an art, and a learned behavior. I'd like to see every mother teach her daughter love muscle control, as she will learn it in this book. The way we respond sexually is a habit. And that's great news—any habit can be unlearned and learned again, just the way you'd like it. That's why the field of sex therapy is growing. So let's see together what early sexual messages *you* picked up.

The following is a small sample of what most of us were taught about sex. Which ones apply to you?

Society's Myths: A Checklist About Sex

Check your dos and don'ts.

DON'T	DO
____Feel sexual	____Remain a virgin until marriage
____Be too forward	____Be dependent
____Be loose	____Be passive

DON'T	DO
____Lose your reputation	____Keep your body powdered and perfumed
____Touch "down there"	____Be ladylike
____Get pregnant until married	____Wait for a man to ask
____Kiss on the first date	____Use sex as a bargaining tool
____Believe anything a boy tells you	____Be attractive
____Swear	____Be monogamous
____Complain	____Have a good figure
____Compete with men	____Marry for money first, then for love
____Masturbate	____Build the male ego
____Depend on men for birth control	____Fake orgasm
____Talk about sex	____Expect a man to know all about sex
*Total*____	*Total*____

Dos and Don'ts Analysis

Some dos and don'ts you have checked may still seem valid to you today. Yet many of these early messages foster fear, guilt, and dependency.

If you show a high score (over eight in each category), some of these ideas are still with you. You may be limiting your potential for sexual pleasure. Your score of dos and don'ts shows you the extent of the influence of your early sexual conditioning. Once you recognize the nature and influence of your conditioning, you can begin to free yourself. Many times at workshops, when women confront and acknowledge their own myths, they are helped. For example, one day when we explored myths about masturbation, Hope said, "I could never let myself do something like that, touch myself. But I guess that's why I let the water do it in the shower. Now I see it's normal, I feel okay about it." It is truly okay to want to explore your sexual self.

Your Sex History

How did your sexual myths affect what happened in your life? In medicine, when you go to a doctor, he takes a physical history to help you. In sexuality, too, there is a history. Let's take a look at what you've gained and experienced. Remember, no one but you will see this record.

First, set aside some time for yourself. For so many women, that's the hardest thing of all to do, but try to find a few minutes to yourself. Loving yourself means taking time alone.

Second, read through the whole group of questions.

Then, fill in brief responses, one- or two-sentence answers. This questionnaire is the same as those used in my workshops, and it has been my experience as a therapist that it is a powerful tool. We each have our own special story in life. The questions you are about to answer are designed to trigger your emotions. They are deliberately personal questions that ask you to remember the primary experiences that formed *you* as a sexual person.

After you have written your replies, you will see what some other women have said.

YOUR SEX HISTORY

1. Your first sexual memory_____

_____

2. Your first experience with menstruation_____

_____

3. Your first experience with masturbation_____

_____

4. Your first experience with orgasm_____

_____

5. Your first experience with intercourse_____

_____

Here are sample answers of other women with which to compare your own.

First Sexual Memory

I felt a special closeness with my Dad. It was nonphysical. We were soulmates. Then I saw an old home movie of myself really flirting with him and licking a lollipop at the same time. [This woman felt a great sense of shame about sex.]

I loved sliding down the bannister at home—it reminded me of a giraffe's neck, and every afternoon when school got out, when I was six or seven, I'd rush home and play my special jungle game—that meant riding the giraffe.

Playing doctor with my cousin. We'd dress up as grownups and set up a "real" office in our playroom. He'd examine me and I'd examine him. It was fun.

I was eleven and my girlfriend and I went horseback riding. I loved the feeling I felt as my thighs gripped the sides of the saddle—I was turned on, but I didn't know it!

A "bad girl" from reform school was hired by my parents as a "mother's helper." She was about eighteen years old. She excited me, told me about sex and got me to play with her genitals and breasts.

I only recall a vacant space, like an empty void; masturbation I guess would be my first sexual memory.

First Experience With Menstruation

I was thrilled and excited. My mother had prepared me for my period when I was ten, but I didn't have my first one until I was sixteen. Everyone was happy at home and I felt warm and content.

It was very embarrassing. My mother called me into the bathroom and showed me a pair of my underpants which had a brown stain in the crotch; she'd found them in the laundry. She was nervous and tried to explain, but I can't remember what she said. I do remember how repulsed I felt when she put a *Kotex* on me—I felt like a baby being diapered.

It happened in gym, and I didn't want to tell anyone, even my mother. I kept my period a secret for about six months. Somehow, menstruation symbolized the death of my freedom as a person. I didn't want to face being a woman, it hurt.

I told my mother and she slapped me, which is our (cultural) custom but I felt humiliated. I didn't want my father to know. I withdrew from men at that time. I felt they could see inside of me.

I loved the heaviness and tension in my pelvis. I felt more alive.

First Experience With Masturbation

I started around twenty, when I had feelings inside my vagina. I put my finger inside but I didn't have an orgasm for about another year, after I read about stimulating my clitoris. Once I was in my room with my mother and one of my sisters. I was lying on the bed and pulling one of my inner lips through a hole in my panties. My mother's harsh disapproval is my main memory.

I first masturbated in high school, after dates, once a week.

I remember staying in from recess when I was in the first grade. I had this aching yet pleasant sensation around my vagina. When all the students left I laid my head on my desk and rubbed my vagina back and forth on the smooth wooden chair. It was wonderful.

I remember masturbating in my crib.

I was thirty-six the first time I masturbated.

My first experience with masturbation was when I was twelve. I had heard somewhere that women could give themselves sexual pleasure and I just kept searching between my legs until I found something that felt good. And then I just kept pressing it. Then I started to shake and felt this incredible feeling, and it was and is the end of the earth. . . . It is one of the most wonderful things that has ever happened to me in my entire life.

First Orgasm

I was twenty-one. I had read my parents' sex manual, and I followed the instructions to stimulate my clitoris and vagina at the same time. I came very fast—I was amazed—so that's what I've been reading about! I love it, but my main memory is of having curiosity satisfied. [This woman had had orgasms with intercourse about three times in her life. She felt she had a sexual dysfunction and was relieved to find out she was just like many other women.]

A man manipulated my clitoris. He was gentle, a giver. I didn't know it was an orgasm. I lost contact with reality, it was so neat, I was completely spaced out—I saw stars.

Wonderful.

Oblivion.

Melting away, letting go totally, release.

First Experience With Intercourse

I was twenty-four. I'm a stewardess. We were flying, it was animalistic—no attachment. I felt guilty.

I was twenty, in junior college, in a friend's apartment. I didn't have any awareness of self-stimulation. It was utter, complete relaxation—I didn't want anything to disturb it—no noise, just lie there and let it wash over me.

Your sex history stands on its own merits as a document of your life. It also shows some of the sex-negative sides of the culture we were all raised in. Your sex history has affected your sexual response pattern. For example, some responses show that women felt so negative about their bodies they avoided contraception. Some women wouldn't use a diaphragm because they were afraid of putting their fingers inside their vagina.

Review the answers to your sex history quiz and rate each response as pleasant or unpleasant.

If you have recorded that you had *three* to *five* pleasant experiences, Hallelujah! You're probably one of the few who did have that many. The information and techniques in this book may be easier for you to absorb than for most women. I hope to help you become an expert.

If you have had more unpleasant than pleasant experiences at these crucial points in your history as a woman, join the club! Go back and read your responses. Then lay this book aside and allow yourself five minutes to get in touch with how you feel. It's not unusual when taking a sex history for responses to pull strings to unpleasant emotions. That's okay. It's important to be in touch with any and all of your feelings, but especially those about your body.

Most women never felt comfortable with their sexuality as they grew up. The picture is one of abuse, incest, and shame. If that has been your history, you have much in common with many others. The fact that you have truthfully faced your memories gives you the option to change.

Take five minutes to dwell on your feelings. Then, let's get together and acknowledge the past, let go of it, and focus on your present.

What They Never Taught in School: A Little Sex History

Now that you've had a chance to consider your own sexual history and how it affects you, it can be enjoyable to take a look at the history of sexuality that provides us with our societal framework. The history of sex has really been a history of orgasm control. Although it's rarely mentioned, orgasm control has again and again been central to historical movements in general as well as to sexual history.

All cultures set taboos around sexual behavior—we're no exception. But some cultures exalt active sexual behavior. They incorporate sexual behavior in religious beliefs. The long history of orgasm control goes back through most of the world's older cultures. It is both surprising and fascinating.

For one thing, the ancient rituals practiced by various cultures fall in line with the latest scientific information. In almost all of them the focus of sexual behavior was mastery of the pelvic muscles. The nineteenth-century explorer Richard Burton wrote of the Indian culture that a woman with sexual skills "is an artist called by the Arabs 'a holder.' Slave dealers pay large sums for such a woman. All women," he added, "have more or less the power but they wholly neglect it." The fine art of lovemaking has been developed, among the Hindus, Taoists, and Japanese, based on control of the pelvic muscles as well as of thoughts and breathing patterns. I'm going to introduce you to these basic techniques of biofeedback as your love muscle exercises.

Among African tribes, building strength with the pelvic muscles was and is currently practiced for both pleasure and health. In one tribe, no girl can marry until she is able to exert strong pressure with her vaginal muscles. In another, women can't leave the birthing hut until they can firmly grasp a finger with their vaginal muscles.

In Western culture physicians such as Hippocrates and Soranus (110 A.D.) tried to aid what they perceived as "hidden injuries" to the pelvic muscles. Early sexologists like the Dutch gynecologist T. H. Van deVelde, writing in 1923, noted that after women had been taught to use their muscles and did so, they reported that they liked sex more and that their sexual functioning, in terms of both frequency and pleasure, was improved.

It's little known that several movements in America were founded on the idea of sexual control. The Utopian Oneida Community was founded in 1848 by John Humphrey Noyes, who advocated male orgasm control. Noyes recognized that the pleasures of sex and the creation of children were separate events, and he wanted them separated as a means of birth control. During intercourse the man was to completely withhold his orgasm. After the woman climaxed, he would gradually let his erection and desire diminish (coitus reservatus). Boys were introduced to this art at puberty by older women of the community. Girls were similarly instructed at a later age by the older men. About the only thing we have left from this group now is the Oneida silver they created.

Coitus reservatus had another run of popularity around 1896, when a physician, Mrs. Alice Bunker Stockham, published a book advocating a lovemaking technique she called karezza. Her book was very popular with female readers and went through many editions. She said that couples who practice karezza will experience "exquisite exaltation." Intercouse should be restricted to a "quiet motion" and orgasm avoided by both parties. Then, in the course of an hour, the physical tension subsides, spiritual exaltation increases, and "visions of a transcendent life are seen."

Next on the enlightened sexuality scene is someone we might take a little more seriously, a turn-of-the-century physician named Robert Dickinson, who started the line of research in sexual physiology later explored by Masters and Johnson. Dickinson reported that he could identify women likely to fail sexually by examining them. "The size, power reactions, and rhythm of contraction of pelvic floor muscle gives information about vaginal types of coital orgasm," he noted. "Many women, after instruction," he added, remarking how important he felt the observation was, "felt what they call orgasm when they failed to before instruction."

It's clear that a few physicians figured out the connection between pelvic musculature and orgasm, yet their findings were ignored or called bizarre by the scientific community. It wasn't until 1966, when William Masters and Virginia Johnson published *Human Sexual Response*, that researchers began to test theories about sexuality.

In my estimation, the parent of the modern understanding of sexuality is Dr. Arnold Kegel. His ideas about orgasm being intensified by a strong love muscle were ahead of his time. Why didn't the medical community rush to adopt Dr. Kegel's ideas? There appears to be some resistance to nonsurgical procedures like exercise among surgeons, perhaps because they are not trained to give preventive medicine, but only to repair by surgery. A colleague of Dr. Kegel, Dr. Robert Scott, whom I interviewed, told me that Kegel "was a bit insulted that his colleagues sloughed off his findings as irrelevant," but he kept on prescribing his exercises.

With the new interest in fitness as a life-prolonging activity, a pelvic exercise program can now come into its own. Against this background there has been an explosion of sexual information—most of it about women—from both theorists and physiologists.

The Twentieth-Century Orgasm Quiz

The sticky wicket in female sexuality in the twentieth century has been misinformation. Take the following quiz to update your knowledge.

THE TWENTIETH-CENTURY ORGASM QUIZ

Incorporating sixteen different current theories of orgasm (an admittedly biased questionnaire).

1. Freud claimed that if a woman had a vaginal orgasm, that meant that she had a mature feminine ego.
   True_____ False_____
2. Orgasm is a total body response.
   True_____ False_____
3. The goal of sex is to have an orgasm.
   True_____ False_____
4. A woman's orgasm depends on her clitoris being stimulated.
   True_____ False_____
5. It takes women much longer to have an orgasm than men.
   True_____ False_____
6. Most women have orgasm during intercourse.
   True_____ False_____

7. You know when you have an orgasm when the following common signs occur:
   a) rise in breathing and pulse rate and blood pressure
   b) hardened nipples
   c) skin flush
   d) sudden release of body tension
   e) curled toes
   True_____ False_____

8. A woman can learn to have orgasm through masturbation.
   True_____ False_____

9. Women enjoy sex as much as men.
   True_____ False_____

10. There is an emotional and mental component to orgasm.
    True_____ False_____

11. The type of orgasm a woman has varies, depending on the tone of her pelvic muscles.
    True_____ False_____

This quiz is "scored" through explanation and sharing information. In fact, many of the answers are both true and false simultaneously. Others are true for one woman and false for another, while some can be true at one time and not at another. After reading the answers you'll be able to rate yourself on new facts learned, self-knowledge gained, and options available. I hope you'll also have a clearer picture of what we know about orgasm in the twentieth century.

1. Q. Freud claimed that if a woman had a vaginal orgasm, that meant she had a mature feminine ego.

A. True. As mentioned before, Freud, who gave

us the concept of an unconscious life, also left us with the idea that "anatomy is destiny." He evolved a complex theory that women developed through two types of orgasm. One kind was centered around the clitoris; it was the type little girls felt when they touched "down there." The second kind came from the vagina, and it was a fulfilling orgasm women had during sexual intercourse with a man. He believed a woman "graduated" to vaginal orgasm; she was expected to leave the "immature" clitoral orgasm behind her. In retrospect, for all his commitment to helping those he treated, Freud's focus on the vaginal orgasm was harmful. The shame of his theory was that women were just seen as dolls: if a woman couldn't experience a vaginal orgasm, she was not fully female and mature. This value judgment, based on a few case studies and extended to the masses, gave women another dose of guilt. How many could identify the source or site of their orgasm, its "normality"? Germaine Greer summed it up when she said, "Freud is the father of pschoanalysis. It has no mother."

2. *Q. Orgasm is a total body response.*

A. True. Sexologists like myself train so they can help women become aware of their entire body as an erogenous zone. After all, the skin is the body's largest sensory organ. And orgasm happens most frequently when our skin is stimulated in the way that we like. For some, that feeling is a prerequisite to becoming orgasmic. Touch is essential. Other women don't need a great deal of tactile stimulation; for

them, it's only a pleasant addition to genital stimulation. In some women who have been measured in
sex labs during orgasm, what they say has been
verified— everything changes, they have a total body
response. For others, nothing measurable changes
significantly. And for some women orgasm changes
from minute to minute, according to the stimulus.
Extreme individual variation is a constant in our new
(non-)model of female sexuality. My point is that
your orgasm is unique, because only you can feel it.
One of the joys of writing this book, what really
counts, is that I may help you to appreciate your own
style of sexual response.

3. *Q. The goal of sex is to have an orgasm.*

A. True and False. True, we are a goal-oriented
society. In our culture we focus on the product, and
in sex, we're told, the product is orgasm. But false,
because the pleasurable process leading to the Big O
in the Sky is discounted and ignored. An example of
the Western focus on orgasm is the word *climax*.
Climax is a vestigial puritanical term that expresses
attaining a peak, which implies an end. Once achieved,
pleasure-seeking behavior is quickly put on the shelf.
This applies to both men and women. However,
when people come for sex therapy, the goal of orgasm is immediately removed. Sex therapy has been
effective when the goal is removed, because there is
no pressure to perform. In the classic exercises of
Masters and Johnson, called "sensate focus," the patient is instructed not to have any orgasms for a
certain number of sessions. The exercises ask you to

give total attention to only one sensory stimulation at a time. The patient and partner are encouraged to enjoy receiving pleasurable sensations from every part of their bodies, *except* their genitals at first. Frequently, clients report orgasm from normally nonerogenous zones. By focusing on the here and now they expand their capacity to receive pleasure. It is my aim for you to discover that it is the moment that matters.

Sensate-focus and other nondemand exercises (that is, ones that involve giving and receiving pleasure without expectation of orgasm, without putting any pressure on yourself), along with relaxation therapy, are the basis of sex therapy. Orgasm is not the goal. I don't want sex to have a goal, just your enjoyment of your body.

Sex therapy is the first practice in psychology that actually has the patient doing exercises. It tries to alleviate sexual dysfunction by short-term (time-limited) therapy. Its importance is that the techniques you learn can be applied to other areas of your life.

4. Q. A woman's orgasm depends on her clitoris being stimulated.

A. True and false. A recent discovery has once again blasted the monolithic theories of Masters and Johnson. Women can and do have orgasms without clitoral stimulation. Masters and Johnson stated that all female orgasms come from the clitoris, that they are all the same, whether the stimulation is direct or, in the case of intercourse, indirect stimulation. But

Dr. John Huffman of Northwestern University reports that women who have had total clitorectomies for medical reasons (and who had experienced orgasm in intercourse *before* the clitoris was removed), report that they *still* experience orgasm. At the time Dr. Huffman did this research, no one wanted to hear that there was an orgasm that could come from vaginal stimulation.

Radical supporters of the women's liberation movement had already focused on the clitoris as the pleasure center. The vaginal orgasm became a myth. Given the problems women had suffered in the name of "normal" orgasm, the emphasis was tremendously freeing. But the majority of women want to come with their partner inside them—and they report sensations of orgasm from inside. Some women sometimes still desire forceful thrusting.

Most women, if asked, report that their orgasm falls somewhere in between—that is, if they can count on having one at all. And that's the point! Sexual information so far has simply not described their experience, or given them any concrete way to know that they will reach orgasm when they want to, in whatever way. I want a woman to be able to come from choice. I want to stress cooperation with yourself, not competition with other women.

5. *Q. It takes women much longer to have an orgasm than men.*

A. True and false. Kinsey found that women can come as rapidly as men. He reported that three-quarters of the men he interviewed reached orgasm within two minutes after penetration, and many in less than a minute. Women who masturbated had orgasms as quickly. However, based on the research since Kinsey, I believe it depends on when a woman first started having orgasms. Sex is a learned response, a habit. You are making, in sex, a basic connection between the mind and the muscle, and some women have never learned how to do that. In general, it takes such women longer to establish the habit. But the whole point is that we are all different: the thing is to avoid "stereotypic patterns of orgasm," in the phrase of sex therapist Marilyn Fithian. What matters is that the exercises and knowledge I give you *intensify and prolong* your orgasm.

6. Q. *Most women have orgasm during intercourse.*

A. False. Statistics say no. The Hite Report said that only 30 percent of women have orgasm with intercourse. Sex researchers Tavris and Sadd in *The Longest War* (Carol Tavris did the *Redbook* Report) estimate that only 25 percent of women are orgasmic with intercourse. These statistics are supported by the pioneering research of Masters and Johnson, who reported in 1966 that female orgasm is triggered only by clitoral stimulation.

I believe that we have been programmed as to how to respond sexually. Most women don't know what their own pattern would be if they had a choice because our culture doesn't teach women to recognize sexual arousal. Hite said that 92 percent could achieve orgasm successfully with masturbation. She also reported a high incidence of women who were multiorgasmic. After that, the pressure was on. Women had to be multiorgasmic, and men had to bring them there. Hite's evidence, however, was based on an extremely limited sample.

The *Redbook* Report, a much better study, said that some women *regularly* have orgasm during intercourse. It also found that women generally limited their masturbation to periods when their partner was away.

That's another model, or stereotype. This book's purpose is to free you—to release you from the repression of even these recent models. We can't be like anybody else. We each have our own unique orgasmic response. Why feel guilty if you don't have multiorgasms? You have your own special way of responding, depending on where your pleasure zones lie. I hope that you realize that all women aren't alike. Here you have freedom from comparison. I give you permission to explore yourself.

7. *You know you have an orgasm when the following signs occur: breathing and pulse rates and blood pressure rise; hardened nipples; skin flush; sudden release of body tension; curled toes.*

A. Hogwash. There are certain scientific measures of orgasm; one is increased heart rate, but even that varies with how athletic you are! Sexual physiologists believe that the only variable in having multiple orgasm is using the PC muscle. Other sexologists say there is hormonal release with orgasm, and some record uterine, even ovarian contractions. But as for overt signs, other than clinically measurable contractions of the love muscle, whether you have had an orgasm or not is subjective.

8. Q. A woman can learn to have orgasms through masturbation.

A. True. That's the basis of treatment for women who do not have orgasms. I am now adding another, the program of love muscle exercises presented in this book.

9. Q. Women enjoy sex as much as men.

A. True. Recent evidence supports this idea. But let's say true *if* they're given a chance.

10. There is an emotional and mental component to orgasm.

A. I think women have always known this. Biofeedback expert and sex researcher John Perry says, "What is important in sex is good neurological connections between the thought processes and the PC muscle." That's the state of the art in sexuality research. Perry shows new physiological evidence for many nerve pathways from several sites within the pelvis to the brain. To him, the point is that these responses, in women as well as men, are controllable.

11. Q. The type of orgasm a woman has varies, depending on the tone of her pelvic muscles.

A. True. I should say so! It has been definitively shown that women who have orgasms with intercourse have stronger PC muscles. The studies make it plain that *women who didn't have any orgasms had the weakest muscles of all!*

Do you know that many people who are in fantastic physical condition have weak love muscles? You don't have to be an athlete to have a strong love muscle. Studies show that women definitely get sexually aroused by contracting their muscle.

Do you see what this can mean for you? In the next chapter I will bring you closer to making all the connections, by helping you explore what you think of your own body.

Keeping Your Love Muscle Journal

Why keep a journal at all? I believe it is very helpful. Behavioral studies show that people who keep written records of their progress are four times more successful than people who don't. Writing down what you do reinforces the activity you performed by giving you immediate feedback. Your journal is also a tangible sign of your commitment. It makes you aware of what you are or aren't doing, and how you feel about it. Your entries can be as short, or as long and descriptive as you desire.

Put the journal where you won't miss seeing it. For example, hang it up, or put it next to your bed, with a pencil handy. In some cases, you may wish to keep your record private.

Your journal can be both useful and enjoyable. It's a record you can look back on—you will enjoy seeing your progress and how you feel about it.

Divide a page into two columns, as follows: "Actions" and "Emotions." Under the "Actions" column list the sexual activity or exercise performed. Under the column labeled "Emotions," describe the feelings—joy, anger, surprise—you experienced at that time. For example:

Actions
Date: 7/22 I did the bathroom test and located my love muscle.

Emotions
It really surprised me. I felt pleased it was under my control.

For now, however, fill in some general notes. There is a pattern to sexual satisfaction and success. The clients who have made the greatest progress in the shortest period of time on this program made a personal commitment to keep their journals up to date. Commitment and interest are part of setting up your new habits.

Let's start now.

My purpose in doing these exercises_____
_____
(Health reasons, improve my sexual pleasure, learn everything I can)

What part of my sexual history was the most important?_____

Why_____

Am I orgasmic?_____

What are my thoughts about exploring new sexual paths?_____
_____

One client, Leslie, kept a journal of her progress in sensual enhancement. Here are some sample entries:

> My purpose in doing these exercises is to intensify my orgasm. I want to know all the skills I can learn. What part of my sexual history was the most important? It was my first orgasm. Why? It was such a release, I didn't know my body could feel so good. I wanted to repeat it. How would I characterize my sexual response pattern? I often use fantasies, I tease myself a lot. It differs if I masturbate or have intercourse. I come fairly rapidly, and I love penetration.
>
> Am I orgasmic? Yes.
>
> What are my thoughts about exploring new sexual paths? It's exciting, and it scares me. My intention is to start from one place and arrive in a more satisfying place.

Your unique sexual response pattern is made up of:

Your definition of sex (what you think sex is)

Your sex history (your experience)

Your values and belief system

The shape and condition of your love muscle

Your capacity for pleasure

CHAPTER 2

Preparation for Orgasm

Body Image and
Your Sexuality

Welcome to a new world, one in which you can separate the parts of sexuality and learn to understand them. Here you can prepare not just your body for orgasm, but your mind.

The connection between mind and body begins with what you think of your body. That affects your sexuality. If you don't like your body or some specific part of it, you become uncomfortable with the idea of sex, or even feel you don't deserve an orgasm. Sexuality training exercises in this chapter will help you become receptive to the idea of physical exercises that lead to orgasm. These exercises work via the mind, because your sexuality is, of course, a matter of the mind as well as muscle.

Getting Naked

Usually in sensual enhancement workshops we reach a point at which everyone, preceded by the leader, has the option to remove her clothes. Nudity alone or in a social context helps people accept themselves and their bodies. Abraham H. Maslow, a pioneer psychologist, said of nudity, "simply going naked before a lot of other people is itself a kind of therapy, especially if you can be conscious of it, that is if there's a skilled person around to . . . bring things to consciousness."

During these sessions amazing things happen. Many thin or average women dread being overweight, and some view themselves as fat because of their deep anxiety about their desirability as females. Taking their clothes off and hearing what other women think of their bodies can radically change behavior.

Your aim here is to acknowledge what has seemed negative about your body and face those feelings. Once you do that you can focus on your body's positive aspects. If you accept the negative elements realistically, they often prove insignificant when viewed within a total context.

Certainly the actuarial tables by which most women were judged overweight are now being overhauled and revised upward to take body types into account. A small backlash against thinness has even begun; the *Journal of the American Medical Association* reports that there is no satisfactory medical definition of obesity, and both the very fat and the very thin have increased mortality rates. You can be cardiovascularly fit and still carry a layer of fat. Therefore an ideal-weight table may not reflect your ideal at all.

What's it like to take your clothes off in a group? Scary at first. Many women fear they can't do it. But after they have gone through the processes of creating a room and relaxed breathing (which I will show you how to do), it becomes possible. When a woman looks at herself naked in a mirror she often expresses astonishment about her body.

In this chapter you will be asked to look at yourself and touch your body. This is essential to unraveling the role society has played in forming your sexual script, or identity. You'll also be asked to think about each body part and take time to note your speech patterns and body movements. How you talk and walk tells the world something about who you are, too. For example, the next time you are at a party, listen to women's conversation. Studies have shown that women tend to place a question mark after a statement, or use words to indicate nonassertive or tentative positions. How do you think other people react to your appearance and manner? Can that have as much to do with your self-image as your body? When a woman does speak assertively she frequently meets with dislike on the part of others.

Letty Cotten Pogrebin, ruefully surveying the gains of the women's movement, remarked, "Boys seldom make passes at female smart-asses." However, assertiveness is necessary. It involves a legitimate request or statement. You have to be able to say what you want in sexuality.

It's also good to feel free to joke about sex. It helps us get through barriers. Each of us has pleasure barriers, marked by a flood of excuses about why one experience or another can't be undertaken. In "pre-orgasmic" groups, for women who have never had an orgasm, these barriers reach a crescendo: there are the kids, they keep banging on the door; there are meetings, and family emergencies, and no alternate time. Find the time. You have a right to your pleasure. Give yourself permission to explore your body.

One reason you may not want to, and I assure you it comes up all the time, is that you think it is dirty to explore your body. I call that the "how disgusting" reaction. Where does that come from? All the early repressive sexual messages that told a little girl not to touch "down there." We were taught in school to keep our pants up and our dresses down. It was drummed into our heads not to talk about our bodily functions with anyone but a doctor. We were also discouraged from asking too many questions about what goes on behind closed bedroom doors, or where babies come from. So many women I have treated tell me that in puberty their body became an incomprehensible enemy, separating them from boys. They dreaded menstruation.

Other women were given the message that sex is something men do *to* them, that the man is responsible for their orgasm. But the key to sexuality is sexual self-responsibility. *You* have a responsibility in sex. You are assuming it by doing the processes in this book. Every chapter will lead you to the goal of control over your own pleasure and pelvic health.

What do I mean by "you have a responsibility"? No one can give you an orgasm; you have to give it to yourself. You must take responsibility and commit yourself to the program.

This is the time to write in your journal:

I commit myself to going through with the body-image process.

Internal Biofeedback

The greatest advance in sexuality has been the introduction of biofeedback techniques to the world of sexual response. Although known for thousands of years to the practioners of yoga, these techniques were only confirmed scientifically about twenty years ago. Since then they have become the basis of a therapeutic explosion. At that time science believed that most body processes were automatic, that you couldn't control them by conscious effort. Dr. Neil Miller shattered that belief by proving he could teach animals and then humans to slow and speed up their heartbeats and lower their blood pressure.

The procedure works on the principle that as you become aware of your bodily processes you can control them. It is now used to stop almost every major bad habit, control high blood pressure, migraines, and skin rashes, and is a recognized treatment for stress attacks. We usually associate biofeedback with machines that beep when you've accomplished a certain body effect, and so give you the feedback. But it is also possible to get feedback internally, which is your goal in this chapter. Behavioral psychologists have discovered that if one is relaxed, any threatening concept one is trying to learn may be approached. This technique is based on the idea that you can't have two competing responses going on in your body at the same time. If you're relaxed, you can't be scared. This concept is used in every major biofeedback clinic, in the desensitization training of people with phobias, as well as in the Lamaze method of childbirth.

I'm going to apply biofeedback techniques to build a solid pleasure base for you. A pleasure base is a substitution of positive feelings for negative ones. It is made up of self-acceptance, self-esteem (what you think), and body awareness (how it feels to be touched). It's a way of making friends with your body.

The Trouble With Hips

Let's see what you think about your body, and how that image was formed. Images of women are defined by the outside world. The models of femininity in our culture are unrealistic. They're also threatening, because they're unattainable. Think of the women in *Playboy* or *Penthouse*. They have very little to do with the everyday life of most women. In a sense we create how we look from these images created by male-dominated industries, and this ideal changes from year to year. In ads for cars and wines, featuring "perfect" women, in cosmetic ads, fashion magazines, on TV, in cigarette ads like those for Virginia Slims, we are told that our sexual attractiveness depends on how we look—almost that our *success* in sexuality will depend on how we look.

Carried to an extreme, the idea that appearance is the key to sexual success causes problems. One woman participant in a workshop told us her feelings about herself depended on male acceptance. "I feel ugly and disgusting when I am rejected," she said. Certainly the current focus on thinness is related to the recent rise in cases of *anorexia nervosa* among teenage girls, a disorder in which a previously healthy adolescent literally can starve herself to death, even going down to sixty-five pounds, still believing herself too fat. It's one of the only psychiatric diseases that is directly life-threatening. Anorexic girls express both fear of having an adult female body and the conviction that they are so fat as to be unsightly.

The most common complaint I hear from women in my workshop is that they are too fat. And where specifically? The part of the body they dislike most is their hips. This quintessentially female part of the body is the one *most disliked* by women.

Depending on keeping us nervous about how we look is a cosmetic industry of 10 billion dollars a year. We are urged to change our hair, face, and nails, and told how they should look. We have to look "perfect."

Often women are encouraged to do "one thing more" to make themselves "perfect." The media push anxiety by using younger and in some instances prepubescent girls to sell products for women (such as in the early Brooke Shields ads, which certainly didn't make most women feel any more comfortable about how *they* looked in jeans).

What's the reality behind this? Many studies show that people feel happier after they have cosmetic surgery they felt was necessary; and the opposite sex does respond favorably to genuine attractiveness. There *is* a reality base to what you think of yourself. The image you have does come in part from innumerable experiences with the real world. You know how people react to you and probably have a good idea of how to make yourself appear more attractive.

The truth is, too, that you face competition with other women. You can't like every woman you meet, and in sex, as well as in business, you may find yourself in head-to-head competition with another woman.

However, your appearance has only *one* meaning *for your sexuality*. That is how *you* feel about it. That statement is so important that it is the basis of the questionnaires in this chapter.

It's very difficult to find any woman who is satisfied with her body. She most often gives as the reason that she is too fat. Is there any basis in fact for this? Certainly we have no reason to love fat. Much of America is either overweight or obese (that is, with too great a proportion of fat), and in women overweight and lack of activity often mean fat settling on the hips. But why then does woman after woman with nothing unusual about their hips call them too fat?

Time and again, no matter what a woman's shape—or what shape she is in—she will focus on her pelvic area negatively. She confesses that her waist, hips, stomach, and thighs are unsatisfactory, or "too fat." Our repressive conditioning about sex has caused many women to deny their sexual feelings, giving them a legacy of "frozen pelvises." The corrosive effect of Victorian ideas of sexuality on women can be illustrated with one quote from a period best-seller, the *Lecture on Chastity* by Sylvester Graham, a lay preacher who invented the Graham cracker. He advised women to pay as little attention as possible to feeling anything from their bodies. "When we are conscious that we have a stomach or a liver from any feeling in these organs," Graham lectured, "we may be certain that something is wrong." Feminist theorists have said that women's absorption of men's fears of them have caused them to take out aggressions on their own bodies.

Because women didn't "feel" much in the pelvic area, gynecologists accepted the mythology that there was no feeling in the pelvis. Doctors are often trained in school that women are naturally anesthetized in the pelvic area. What Dr. Kegel taught with his exercises was how to help the pelvis come alive.

Fatness

In *Fat Is a Feminist Issue*, Susie Orbach says that fat is protection, body armor. It can also be protection against sex. Studies record that fat women are often seen as nonsexual and androgynous. Orbach also calls it a woman's only way to counter suppressed rage, suppressed assertiveness. What is clear is that fat people are definitely discriminated against, most importantly in the workplace. But is being too fat by a standard of society the same issue as you not liking your body, or feeling nonsexual? No. A fat person can be as sexually adept (if perhaps more limited in agility) as a slender one. Not all people who are loved, or even adored as sexual masters, are slender. That's simply not a prerequisite to enjoying sex. What is, is being self-accepting, having self-esteem. Being sexually fit is a separate issue from fatness. In *Such A Pretty Face*, talking about obesity and desexualization, Marcia Millman says, "Taking a good look at oneself—in front of other women or alone—affirms your sex, and sexuality. It also affirms your right to be a woman."

Looking at Yourself

Here are three sketches of bodies, labeled A, B, C.

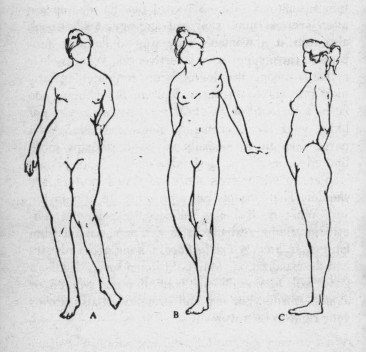

I look like

A) _____   C) _____

B) _____   None of the above _____

The following questionnaire gives you a chance to find out what you feel about your body and to compare your feelings with what other women have answered.

Use a single word or phrase to describe the way you feel about the various parts of your body. Your body profile will give you a clearer picture of how you perceive them. You are going to find the experience of describing your body interesting, educative, and reassuring.

Write this in your journal:

MY OPINIONS ABOUT MY BODY

What part of your body do you like best?_____

Why?_____

What part do you like least?_____

Why?_____

Did you try to rate yourself (being a judge)?_____

Who are your models for physical attractiveness? Models from beauty and fashion magazines? *Penthouse* pets? Your mother? Men?_____

What do your descriptions tell you about how sexual you are?_____
_____

What part of your body do you feel is the most sexual?_____
_____

What parts of your body do you feel are the most useful?_____
_____

What do you want your body to communicate to others?_____
_____

I hope that these questions have helped you feel that what your body communicates to *you* is more important than what it communicates to others.

MY BODY PROFILE

Use a single word or phrase to describe the way you feel about the following parts of your body:

My face_____

My neck_____

My breasts_____

My arms_____

My waist_____

My hands_____

My genitals_____

My legs_____

My hips_____

My thighs_____

My knees_____

My calves_____

My ankles_____

My feet_____

My toes_____

Bodies—In a Word: Interpretations of Your Answers

In the atmosphere of support and trust, let's look at your responses compared to those of other women. As you reread your list, try not to be hard on yourself, try to make no judgments good or bad. No one has a better response than you. Here, then, is what other women feel.

The majority feel good about their bodies. Some say their bodies are "terrific," some just say "okay." The important message is that going by outside appearances, there is nothing to predict how a woman will feel about her body!

Faces, hands, arms, knees, legs, feet, and toes received the most positive response. Here are actual answers. If you described yours favorably, you are in the majority. These areas are not usually emotionally weighted.

My face: Attractive, pretty, delicate, cute, innocent, interesting, changeable, soft, beautiful and sweet, blemished, lined.

My hands: Sensitive, caring, loving, giving, musical, sturdy, strong, sensual, firm, warm, gentle, handy, expressive.

My arms:	Strong, soft, happy, helpful, useful, shapely, tan, muscular, sinewy, graceful, sturdy.
My knees:	Funny, bendable, strong, pliable, wiggly, runner's, sprained, sensual, ugly, knocked.
My legs:	Long, heavy, shapely, muscular, fat, midline point of the body, slim, adequate, tense.
My feet:	Unusual, sensual, expressive, strong, small, walking, short, comfortable, strengthening, pretty, dancer's, sexy.
My toes:	Short, wiggly, long, cute, practical, pretty, manicured, happy, crooked, sexy.

What about your breasts and genitals? It is in these areas that one might expect women's fears of not being perfect to concentrate. But just the opposite is true. If you answered favorably you are in the majority.

My breasts:	Soft, adequate, full, lovely, happy, flaunting, firm, round, small, feminine, cute, nice.

Most women also extolled the virtues of their genitals. What do you feel? By the end of the book, come back and answer this again. Has the answer changed?

My genitals:	Sweet, delicious, pleasing, lovable, beautiful, small, mysterious, moist, willing, open, delicate, unexplored, mine, sensitive.

Women who gave negative descriptions were few, but those who did focused on their guilt feelings, using such words as *sick*, *shameful*, *disgusting*, *dirty*, and *smelly*.

The preponderance of positive adjectives about their genitals reveals an accepting side of American women not heard from before.

Then where does the negative feeling focus? On waist, hips, stomach, and thighs. Women called them fat, chubby, ugly, thick, enormous, ample, oversize, heavy, flabby, unattractive, large, a disaster, Jell-O, fat dimples, unfeeling, numb, bulging, lacking awareness, dead.

Did you answer in the same general way? Then you are in the vast majority.

I have come to call this pelvic area the "dead zone." Why? The only way to avoid feeling something from your pelvis *is* to keep it numb. A stiff pelvis is stiff with fear of pleasure, the fear of losing control, of enjoying sex. For example, the same hips one woman described as "horrible" were seen by others in the group as "generous, voluptuous, and sexy." At first when Mary received this information she protested and tried to convince the group that her hips were truly repulsive. Finally, she relaxed and listened to positive feedback and admitted that she liked the fleshy feel of her hips. Unfortunately, her heaviness blocked her sexual enjoyment because she felt unattractive.

Most of us fall somewhere between fat and thin, but we *still* don't accept our bodies. That's because our image of ourselves was formed by someone outside us, and not ourselves.

It can be illuminating to find out, for example, how men feel about the same body areas. In *Sexual Choices*, leading sexologist Roger Libby quotes a *Psychology Today* study that compared women's and men's feelings about their own bodies. Both liked their faces, shoulders, hands, and feet equally well. Men were satisfied with chest/breast (82 percent), while women also showed a high (74 percent) satisfaction. The sexes began to diverge, however, at the abdomen, where 64 percent of men but only 50 percent of women were satisfied. Only 57 percent of women were satisfied with their buttocks, but 80 percent of men were. With thighs, the story became clear. Eighty-eight percent of men were perfectly satisfied, but only 51 percent of women could accept their thighs.

A Tale of Two Bodies

Farrah Fawcett, a woman whose business is her beauty, said, surprisingly, "I find a lot of women 'beautiful' who are not beauties. Women are beautiful when they're doing the thing they do best." Beauty is not the exclusive property of the beautiful or the young. Neither is sexuality.

One summer, years before I became a full-time sex therapist, I made my first visit to Sandstone Ranch, a humanistic growth center high in the hills

outside Los Angeles. This is the Sandstone of Gay
Talese's book *Thy Neighbor's Wife*; at that time it
provided a safe, comfortable atmosphere in which
sex could be freely explored, privately or publicly.
When I went I was determined to learn all I could,
yet I sat by myself in a corner with my palms sweating,
while a voice that sounded remarkably like my
mother's kept repeating over and over in my head,
"What in God's name are you *doing* here?"

I felt my body was the equal of anyone's there, but
I was rigid with the idea that I might have to take my
clothes off. My gaze flitted around the room, then
settled on a large woman who seemed, incredibly, to
be holding court at the other end of the room. Her
clothes were off, mine were definitely on.

There she was, surrounded by an animated group
of people, all relaxed and talking. Her ample nude
body had a healthy glow, and someone burst into a
laugh at the end of one of her stories. They seemed
mesmerized. Slowly I forgot myself and drew nearer,
where I was introduced to Brenda.

Clearly, Brenda loved herself and her body even
with its flaws. She was and is a woman who knows
herself. Forty, fat, and single, she walked naked into
a room full of strangers and enjoyed herself. That's
self-assurance! People are drawn to self-assured
individuals. I wanted to know how she did it.

Over the summer we became friends. She told me
her understanding of herself had not been easy to
come by. It had to be learned. "I didn't get rid of my
past," she explained. "I don't think it's possible. What

I did do was study the programming and scripts I
was raised with."

I've gradually come to accept the idea that we
were indeed raised with scripts for living, when we
were taught as children not to touch "down there."
From that attitude, many women learned to dread
sex. Most women, I have found, still believe in
Grimm's fairy tales, filled with excitement culminat-
ing in happy endings. These scripts don't work in the
real world. They're based on romantic ideals of the
woman using her sexuality to get and control her
partner.

Brenda taught me to avoid scripts by valuing my
body as a friend. Her smile says that although she's
no knockout, she doesn't seem to know it—and, what's
more, neither does anyone else! She is attractive
because she's given up comparing herself to other
women. She has decided what she wants, and naked
or fully dressed, she is her own yardstick and model.
Above all, Brenda is human and sexual.

Years later, on the same day that a high-fashion
model in a workshop told us she hated her body, I
met another woman who understood herself. While I
was preparing this book, I met Jane again. We had
lunch together. Her transformation since the workshop had been phenomenal. She suggested we meet
at one of the brightest, best restaurants in the area.
But when I first met Jane, she weighed 350 pounds.
Her husband had just died; she was a mess, but
determined to learn about the sexuality she had never
had a chance to discover. During the workshop, she
participated in the body-image process, part of which

was the option to undress before the group. To be truthful, I was apprehensive for her. She said it was the hardest moment of her life. But she did it, and the group saw that she was alive, human, and sexual, and we ended up in tears of joy. After the workshop, Jane went to a clinic and lost 100 pounds of life-threatening weight, but she's still heavy. What's really changed is her attitude—she radiates a feeling of calm and self-acceptance.

We have new and better role models now than those presented by the media. We see for ourselves women in their forties and fifties, vital and creating; or young, making their mark on the world. Betty Ford has said, "A liberated woman is one who feels confident in herself and is happy in what she is doing. She is a person who has a sense of self. It all comes down to freedom of choice."

A Room of Your Own

If you really want to create and control your orgasm, especially if you have never or seldom had an orgasm, you must make a commitment of time to the processes in this book. You will need forty-five minutes to an hour per day until the neural connections are made. If you are advanced, you will still need perhaps fifteen minutes a day. The time spent will be worth it. I will also explain how to tie your exercises to daily activities. *Now* is the time to shut the door and block out all distractions.

I invite you to join me on a creative journey. Here you will learn how to handle stress by making a room of your own—your own mental place for relaxation.

First, imagine a very safe, pleasurable, comfortable room. The most effective technique the science of psychology (as well as sports) has devised to teach technique is a kind of mental practice called creative visualization.

Imagine a room in which you create a calm atmosphere. In this room you are safe. It is your retreat. This room is going to be yours whenever you want it. You'll be able to relax there and quietly close the door even in the middle of a busy day. Place the windows wherever you want them; make the room as light or dark as you desire. In your room, surround yourself with fabrics and textures of bright or soft colors, but only those that are pleasing to the touch, putting in it objects that you consider lovely and restful, because they especially are the things you like to touch. Be detailed in your mind—the more exact you are the easier it is to find it in a stressful situation. There are no limits in this magical place.

Now let yourself go. Fill the room with the scent of your favorite perfume or flowers. Savor the smell for a moment . . . mimosa or jasmine on a warm night. Let it linger. Etch it firmly in your memory. Take a moment and fill your sensuous room with your favorite personal things. Music, a cashmere throw, soft cushions, satin sheets. And a glass by your bedside, stemmed, perhaps filled with champagne? How about a tray with a selection of your favorite foods, cognac and caviar, petit fours, steak and a salad? This is your room and you alone are the creator of it. Pictures of those you love, or a wardrobe of clothing you'd love to wear. Books you love, or a scene out the window of where you'd like best to be. Relax and be comfortable with the environment you have created. From this moment onward, this is a room evocative of your sensuality.

In your journal, use a space to describe your room. Writing it down helps to keep the image clear.

Your Sensual Self

Another exercise in creative visualization that yields valuable information is to imagine the ideal you, that is, *your* ideal.

Rest and get comfortable. Close your eyes and look at her. See her body as the one you want to have. Feel her mind as the one you wish to have, feel her sensuousness as yours. She is a part of you, although you may have denied her existence. She is your friend, your sexuality. Take a moment to build all the parts of her figure. Think about her in detail, answering such questions as

What color hair does she have?

What color eyes?

How long is her hair?

What is her skin tone?

What is her height, weight, bone structure, shoe size, breast shape?

What nationality is she? What race? How old is she?

What is the tone of her voice?

What sorts of things does she say?

Take a few minutes and complete the creation of your sensuous self.

If you could describe her in one word, what would it be?_____

Now, open the door to your hideaway and invite her in to join you.

Open your eyes when ready.

During my workshops, several women shared their visions of their sensuous woman with me. Sara described her sensuous woman as "so beautiful that I might lose my head and fall in love with her." Meagan said, "I want to create that private woman whenever I make love." "The image of my sensuous woman is so powerful that all I want to do is strive to reach her level of sexuality. This means I never have to feel alone," Lauren said. "I see sunlight, and realize I can ride through life by trusting myself."

All the women who created their sensuous woman reported loving her, but some were afraid of her. Women who were afraid said their hesitation to let her into their room, to join her on what she promised, a journey of sexual exploration, was based on their fear of sexuality and the unknown. It's okay and natural to feel scared. The most important thing is to go ahead, trust yourself. The first necessary step in sexuality is to face yourself sexually. Take this at your own pace, and enjoy it. All of the exercises in this book are designed to show you that your sexuality is nothing to be afraid of. In your private room you will feel free to explore yourself.

See Me, Feel Me, Touch Me

Researchers have found that relaxation techniques, the techniques of breath control used in biofeedback, are the first things that need to be done when a person has something new to learn. Behavioral psychological studies show that if you relax, no matter how threatening the idea, as long as you control your breathing you can't stay scared of it. The reason is that if you feel relaxed you cannot simultaneously feel afraid.

Once you can control breathing, therefore, you can become your own biofeedback system.

To start the process you must learn first how to both tense and relax every body part, and how to control breathing. If you tense up voluntarily, you soon learn to identify it when it is happening *in*voluntarily, in response to stress. What are the signals of stress? Rapid breathing, muscle tension, rapid speech, tone of voice changing, clenched teeth and fist, increased pressure in the chest. You may also become pale or start to sweat.

Stress management is a relatively new branch of medicine, but it rests on the concept that you can control what is happening to your muscle tension and your breathing— and therefore control the damaging effects of stress. In the next exercises you will learn how to create this foundation for controlling breathing and musculature. This training will allow you to identify your stress reactions. Then you are already trained to retreat into your breathing, which you regularize, and to find (in a split second) the quiet, serene, nurturing room of your own. This method allows you to center yourself, and back you come, focused and calmer. In a way it is a form of self-hypnosis. It is as useful for the stock analyst as for the teacher, banker, secretary, dancer, lawyer, or mother.

To begin learning these biofeedback techniques, find some time to relax. Take the phone off the hook and close the door. For starters, take a soak in a hot tub. This is a recipe for relaxation. Make the tub or shower a different kind of experience for you. Use a different texture of towel, a new sponge, a new scent. Buy a flower and put its petals in your bath. Please yourself.

After your bath, lie down and find a comfortable position. Stretch out. Stretch your body. Move around and make this space your own. Allow the tensions of the day to melt away.

Close your eyes and become aware of your body. Take a slow trip from the top of your head to the tips of your toes, becoming aware of any tenseness as you focus on each part of your body in turn. Notice any physical sensations or feelings that take place. Take yourself outside yourself and observe your feelings. Don't let negative thoughts get in the way—observe them silently and watch them slip away. This may be the first time you have taken real time with yourself, with your body. Women are so often the ones who give to others, to children, husbands, parents. Now give to yourself. Allow yourself to do this process in security.

Beginning with the muscles of your face, tense and relax your muscles. Tighten them into a grimace. Pull your shoulders up around your ears . . . tighter . . . now let them go. Tighten your upper arms, your forearms, make your hands into fists. Tighten and let go. Begin to feel your face and shoulders and arms grow heavy and sink toward the floor. Now focus on your spine. Make it rigid and tight . . . tighter . . . now let your spine go. Tighten your buttocks, your thighs, your calves. Tense the muscles in your feet now . . . tense them up and now let them go. Begin to feel your back and spine growing heavy and sinking toward the floor. Your whole body is feeling heavy and is totally supported by the floor or bed beneath you.

Breathe. Focus your attention on your breathing. Start breathing deeply from your abdomen, and focus on your breath. As you inhale, your abdomen rises or expands; as you exhale it should fall. This pattern of pushing up the diaphragm to expel breath (make the body space smaller) and lowering the dia-

phragm (allowing the lungs room to expand) is basic
to all athletic exercise. You will have learned it already if you are a runner. It is designed to get the
maximum amount of oxygen into the body, and as
rapidly as possible to the muscles.

Place your right hand slightly beneath your bellybutton and breathe deeply from your abdomen. Inhale.
As you inhale, your hand should push up as your
diaphragm expands, increasing the volume of air you
take in. Exhale. Push the exhalation out with your
diaphragm. Feel it glide past your lips. The hand
resting easily on your stomach should ease back to its
original position.

Concentrate on this quiet breathing rhythm for ten
breaths. The feeling is not exercise, but becoming
aware of a variety of sensations. Tense and contract,
feel air going past your lips, feel the beginnings of
little sexual stirrings, and let them turn you on.

At the next five inhalations, say to yourself, "I
deserve to understand and love my body." Don't
think about how silly it might feel, just do it. In the
beginning of this process, most clients report they
feel awkward.

Here are some of the shadows that may flicker by
in your mind. Be the observer, watch them and let
them go by. Here are quotes from other participants:

> This is the most stupid thing I've done in a long
> time. I've got a million other things I could be
> doing, like defrosting the refrigerator, watering
> the garden, writing to my sister. What the hell am
> I doing lying on the floor breathing?

I've got a meeting tonight. Anything could help me more than this exercise. What does breathing and relaxation have to do with my having an orgasm anyway?

Why do I keep seeing myself as a little girl waving goodbye to my mother as I carry my lunchpail off to school?

I wish I could share this with some of my friends, but they'd think I was wasting my time. I mean, a grown woman should know all she needs to know about sex, right?

Am I really going to learn something new about myself? What would my husband think if he found out what I was doing?

But after the process, the same women said:

I was very nervous before I did this exercise; however, I am not nervous now.

I feel I have learned a lot about who I am and what I take time for and what I don't: I feel I know myself better.

I've never felt so relaxed in my life. Boy, will I sleep tonight.

As you exhale the next five times, imagine that your breathing is like gentle waves on a shore and that each wave is slowly washing away the last ten-

sions from your body. Let all negative and judg-
mental thoughts pour out of your body like stale,
toxic air. You have no use for them, their vitality is
gone. By pushing them out you are making room for
new information and attitudes to be absorbed and
reinforced.

Mirror Images: My Naked Self

No one can change with a negative self-image, so
you must look at and touch this body you have been
describing. Your inner image is tied to your image of
your body, but there is no other way to accept it
other than to touch it.

Breathing sensually, and easily, stand naked in
front of a mirror. Don't rush. Take the time and
concentrate. You may become increasingly turned
on. It is a natural reaction. But feeling the sensation
instead of going for the orgasm can be of more benefit to you now. That is because what you are doing
here is building up pathways for pleasurable sensations,
leading to no goal. It is good here, therefore, to hold
off.

Focus on every part of your body in turn from
head to toe.

Close your eyes and touch your body, then answer
for each part these questions:

How do I feel about this part of my body? (Do I
like it or not? Why?)

What are my fingers feeling? (Rounds, forms, textures. Receive the pleasurable sensations.)

Have I avoided touching any parts of my body? Why?

The theory behind this exercise is to restore you to a higher and more realistic self-appraisal. When you answered whether you like the feeling of touching your body, if you answered negatively about any particular part, you may have old mental or physical traumas associated with it. It is important to realize that these can color your responses to it. Can you touch again and accept it? Focus on what your fingers feel. It is pleasant to touch, and helps you like *all* parts of your body to receive pleasure from them. There are two ways you "see" your body: a mental picture or image of what your body looks like is one; but if you close your eyes and feel those same body parts that you've already described, the image your tactile sense evokes often differs from your visual image. A common example of this is found when women touch their "dead zone" (hips, abdomen, and upper thighs), which they reported as flabby, ugly. When their eyes are closed they say .

It's soft, comforting.

I like the softness.

Gee, maybe it's really okay to say flab . . . it feels like an old fur coat.

Sensory awareness means taking a risk and getting rid of negative programming. To do this we are going to use a self-affirming technique from therapeutic practice, because basic to all risk-taking is self-affirmation. In workshops I always ask clients to say, "I *love myself.*" Client after client, after saying the words, is moved to a deep, significant emotion that appears to be at the heart of self. It is hardest, by the way, for those who are fat to say these words.

Now, perhaps, you can say it. "I love myself," three times, out loud. Are there tears? You are not alone.

The intense emotion that follows acknowledging self-love will speed your self-awareness. It's not easy at first to make this statement. Unfortunately, in the social conditioning process our true and natural feeling of self-love gets distorted. That negative programming has to be altered. Getting to love yourself is part of facing your body and loving all parts of it.

Perhaps now, if you have not already done so, you can say aloud, "I love myself."

You have now looked long, and we hope lovingly, at your body. You have acknowledged that you *can* love yourself. Now you are ready to enjoy the delights of controlling your love muscle.

CHAPTER 3

Making the
Mind-Body Connection

One of the most troublesome ideas in Western civilization is the idea that the mind operates separately from the body. But as sexuality exists entirely in the connection between mind and body, the greatest effect of that central philosophical idea on our civilization has been difficulties with sexuality. In our culture the separation between mind and body has been so great that any connection between the two was treated as if it did not and could not exist. So, neither could sexuality—at least not in polite society. Most of all it could not be understood. We have had to turn to science, a method we trust because it tries to be rational, to prove that there are actual physical connections between the mind, the feelings, and the poor desiring body.

Most of our learning has come via the fields of

psychology and sports physiology. In competitive sports athletes and coaches have learned to make the mind-body connection. They train and control their muscles, breathing, and mental attitudes by the methods I teach you in this book. The result is the basis of the modern splurge of athletic record breaking: athletes have learned to control specific parts of their bodies with their minds. It is a prime method in modern coaching and is done by hooking them to machines in labs, using training films; it is the aim of all Olympic-level workouts.

But the field of sex research itself has also explored the mind-body connection. There has been an explosion of research into sexual physiology, and what we call the mind-body connection.

Orgasm is one function of a strong, working love muscle. What a strong love muscle does is give you pleasure. The pleasure flows via neural connections from your muscle to the rest of your body. These pathways connect thought with sensation, sensation with pleasure, and pleasure with thought. What you are going to do in this chapter and the next is make that connection strong and solid.

What Shape Is Your Love Muscle In?

You're going to focus on what shape your love muscle is in. There will be several objective tests you can do to rate its condition, and a system for rating what level you are at.

Here you will set fitness levels as a practical matter, so that you can set realistic, actual goals for these pragmatic exercises. Two of the tests that follow will tell you how long your exercises will take per day and how long it will be before you can expect to feel the first effects of love muscle exercise. The third will begin to bring in the other aspects of this very special muscle. In it you'll examine its role in creating feelings that lead to orgasm.

In *Arnold: The Education of a Bodybuilder*, Arnold Schwarzenegger, a world champion muscle builder, and a phenomenon of body-building methods in his own right, says, "You must consider that in the beginning you are training the mind as well as the body. The mind, after all, makes you want to train; it turns on the body. Because the mind motivates you to train the body, you have to train the mind first. If the mind doesn't want to lift weights, the body won't lift them."

There is a lot of information behind that idea. In the pelvis there are five sets of muscle groups, of which the love muscle is the major one. These muscles are all connected to the pelvis, which itself is connected to fifty-seven other muscles!

This chapter will turn on the body. The rushing of blood into your muscle when you clench it, the sensations you feel, becoming one with your sensuality, will tune you in to turning on.

Your Fitness Baseline

First you need to set up your sexual fitness baseline, which will tell you at what level to start doing the exercises. You will take two tests:

Your general level of fitness quiz

Your timed love muscle control test

After that you begin the process that culminates in the last test:

The love muscle condition test.

YOUR GENERAL LEVEL OF FITNESS

What is your present state of health?

Excellent_____ (If you are in excellent health you are likely to know it, and are probably quite physically active.)

Good/Fair_____ (If you get at least one cold a year, exercise some, and haven't seen a doctor except for a routine checkup in a year, you are fairly healthy.)

Poor_____ (If you are permanently handicapped, chronically ill, smoke or drink heavily, or have been hospitalized for over one week in the last year, you are in poor health.)

Would you classify your job as
  Physically active (dancer, construction work)_____

  Somewhat active (housecleaning, salesperson)_____

  Sedentary (desk job)_____

Do you have a regular exercise program?_____

  Time per day_____

  Time per week_____

Are you overweight more than 5—10 pounds?_____

10—20?_____ (Can you pinch an inch under your
                    upper arm? An inch on the torso?
More than 20?___ If so, it indicates overweight.)

What sports or activities do you engage in?
  Running_____ Miles daily_____ Weekly_____
  Tennis, squash, racquetball _____
      Singles____ Doubles____ Hours per week____
  Swimming_____ Laps_____ Sprints (interval
  training)_____
  Dance_____ Hours per week_____

  Yoga or other meditative arts_____ Hours
  per week_____
  Martial arts, t'ai chi, etc. _____ Hours per
  week_____
Do you smoke?_____

Analysis of Your Answers to Fitness Assessment

Your answers have probably already revealed to you whether you are fit or not. Now, let's take a closer look at what your answers mean based on the latest fitness information. Rate yourself on two conditions: (1) if you do twenty minutes or more of aerobic activity daily (physically vigorous exercise which makes you breathe heavily and requires more oxygen); or (2) if you exercise aerobically three times a week for 1 ½ hours or more. If you fit into either of these categories, you are physically fit, or committed to becoming so. Check the other factors following to see how your answers affect your fitness. Each of the factors only come into play at various levels.

Overweight. If you are twenty pounds *over-* or *underweight* but exercise daily or have other evidence of cardiovascular competence—such as comfortably running a mile in twelve minutes—you are still fit.

For a current or former athlete, good condition can be maintained on a twenty-minute-per-day schedule, since you already know exactly how to stress and work out your muscles and your heart to the maximum in that amount of time (not counting warmup).

Semiactive or inactive job. If you have a semiactive or inactive job, and exercise is *not* a regular part of your life (for example, it is sporadic and does not include strenuous cardiovascular stress for more than twenty minutes per session), but you do engage in some sport or fitness activity two to three times per week, you are in fair condition.

Regular exercise program. If you formerly worked out sporadically but are now exercising regularly two to three times per week, you may be in the process of taking command of your body and can be considered in fair condition.

Smoking. Diet and sleep are vital, but I can't reach into your living room to analyze them for you. The statistics on smoking, however, are clear. Smoking indicates a fair to poor level of involvement in physical exercise. If you occasionally play sports or do stretching exercises and are in fair condition but smoke, your fitness will actually be poor. If you smoke, rarely exercise strenuously, and have a sedentary job, you are in poor physical condition.

These categories hold no matter what your age. You are probably fit no matter how old if you engage in over twenty minutes of strenuous activity per day regularly (not counting warmup time) and do not smoke. On the other hand, no matter how young you are, even though your muscles may seem quite toned up, you can consider yourself *not* in good physical condition if for the preceding six months you have not worked out in a strenuous job or followed a fitness program including aerobic exercise for twenty minutes at least three times weekly.

If you are in excellent physical condition, you are at Level One.

If you are in good/fair physical condition, you are at Level Two.

If you are in poor condition (not physically active), you are at Level Three.

Note in your journal which level you are at for general physical fitness.

YOUR LOVE MUSCLE CONTROL TEST

The next test will be an assessment of your specific level of love muscle control. In order to begin that assessment, write the answers to these questions:

Were you able to identify your love muscle in chapter 1?_____

How was that experience?_____

Was the love muscle extremely easy to find?
  (I found it the first time I clenched.)__(Level One)

  I found my love muscle with some effort. (I found it the second time I clenched.)_____ (Level Two)

  It was difficult to find. I found it after_____ times. (Level Two)

  I did not find it._____ (Level Three)

After you first clenched your love muscle, did you take that feeling with you at any other time of the day?_____
_____

What did you feel when you contracted it?_____
_____

Does that action bring any mental associations or pictures to your mind's eye?_____

Would you say you can contract your love muscle at will?_____

Did you do so just now?_____Is that feeling becoming familiar?_____ Is it pleasant?_____
Are you comfortable with it?_____ If you clench your muscle at other times, what times are they, and what do you think of at those moments?_____
_____

If you were not able to identify your muscle, have you tried again? How often did you try?_____

Were you able to identify your muscle during the week?_____

If you have not yet identified your muscle are you still willing to try?_____

Don't forget that two-thirds of American women have trouble identifying this muscle!

When you identified your muscle in chapter 1, you simply clenched it while urinating. To get a clearer measurement of your love muscle control do the same thing again, but this time time the flow to see how quickly you can stop it.

Let your bladder get unusually full, then go into the bathroom to urinate. (If this sounds too bad, do the test when you would ordinarily go to the bathroom. The results aren't as revealing, but you will still be able to feel yourself work the muscle and time it.) Take a watch in with you to time the seconds.

Before you begin, take a few seconds to breathe and relax. Taking up a position with the legs spread wide, start the flow of urine, time it, and stop the flow as quickly as you can.

How many seconds of flow did you have before you stopped it? Relax for a moment with the flow stopped; relax your legs. As you do, notice how full you still feel. Would you say your bladder is still three-quarters full, half full, or almost emptied?

Write the seconds it took to stop the flow and how full the bladder was in your journal, with today's date.

The following table gives you a general rating of your love muscle control level based on this test.

Keep in mind that approximately two-thirds of American women have weak pelvic muscles. Don't feel discouraged by your results. Fortunately, even the weakest muscle can be improved amazingly in a few short weeks!

"Good" in the table indicates Level One. "Fair" is Level Two, and "Weak" is Level Three.

Now you have the results of two tests of your love muscle function. It's time to delve deeper into the subtleties of your sexuality.

LOVE MUSCLE CONTROL

Time It Took to Stop Urine Flow	Can You Stop This Much?	Your Degree of Control Is	Your Muscle Condition Is
1–2 seconds	Almost completely full—three-quarters full; it's easy to stop the flow.	*Excellent:* you can probably empty bladder a teaspoon at a time.	Good
3-4 seconds	From just under three-quarters full— just above half full	*Satisfactory:* the urine flow requires effort to stop and some still dribbles out after you squeeze the muscle.	Fair
5-6 seconds	Can't stop the flow until the bladder is half empty.	*Poor:* stopping the flow requires a great deal of effort.	Weak

A Neural Aphrodisiac

It's an exhilarating feeling using your muscle, isn't it? No matter whether it is in good shape or not, what a pleasure to be able to identify it and know that *your muscle for orgasm* is under *your* control! It's a revelation.

The next test for your fitness baseline is as simple as the last two, but it involves getting closer to your sensuality. Here you are not only learning to tune into the body as a sensual network and determining your fitness level, but also determining your sensuality. This is the point at which you must begin thinking *sex*, because without the connection between muscle sensations and sex, there can *be* no orgasm.

When you think about your sexuality in that light, there are no levels. The levels I have given you serve only to "tune you in to turning on"—that's what creates orgasm, because your body is responsive to the play of thoughts in your mind. That's the reason behind the effectiveness of the exercises you've done in creative visualization. They connect sensation to pleasure. You made that connection again when you clenched your muscle in the love muscle control test.

People often contract this muscle involuntarily at many times during the day, for example, when they see someone attractive. As a matter of fact, one problem women have when they begin their exercises is that they feel aroused. There is no doubt that you will feel pleasure whenever you contract your muscle. Don't deny this pleasure. Instead, enjoy it. There is good reason to notice the thoughts you're having when you clench your love muscle.

Two times today, clench your muscle, and notice what your thoughts are. Write them down in your journal. As you note these thoughts, realize it is very important to establish a firm neural connection from your muscle use to your pleasure and to your mind, just the way you built the "room of your own." Later you will do "turning on" exercises that will be associated with tightening your muscle.

When you are about to explore your sensuality, it's very important to set the stage. You'll begin with a process of touching.

Fingertip Touching

Set aside one half hour for this next exercise. To awaken your senses, retreat into your mental room of your own. Think of the space you have set aside for yourself. Then set the stage for yourself, in reality. Thinking of your own warm, welcoming dream room, make your real room as much as possible like it. Create your sensual room in real life. Put soft or satiny sheets on your bed, pour yourself a glass of wine. Think of each of your senses, and include something special to bring each one alive. Buy flowers, eat a favorite food, listen to a lovely piece of music. In this setting you have created your own sensual reality. This is a room in which to make love. You are going to keep those sensations so that when you go out of this room you can always recreate them.

In this warm room, relaxed, you begin to touch your naked body. Prepare yourself for a remarkable experience, for you will be asked not to touch any of the areas that you usually find arousing.

Rub your hands together until they are warm, and

when you touch yourself, close your eyes and sink deeply into the feeling. Feel as if your whole body is focused on your gently moving fingertips. Then slowly and gently place your hand on your hairline and forehead, with no abrupt movements. Your whole purpose here is to form an unbroken circle. Feel your touch and your response to it as a circle. There is no place here for rough or impatient movements. Let your fingers move lightly over your skin and slide delicately over the forehead. As you move smoothly from the hairline to outline the temples and the eyes, sink into the sensation coming from the fingertips. You will feel intensely focused on their movement and the spot that is being touched. It is as though all tension and unhappiness is delicately moved away. Do not massage or wiggle the skin. Do move your fingertips to take the body's attention with them, just the way a magnet in the child's game will move over the glass and take the iron filings with it.

Touch your face and ears, down to your neck and on to the tense muscles at the back of the neck. Only touch with the fingertips; then move on. You can feel yourself becoming soothed. Run your fingertips lightly down your arms; make an outline of your body, up the arms, down the waist, feeling the thighs, tracing the outer side and the tops, but not the inner.

Notice what sensations you are feeling from your fingers and how parts of your body feel and react. Touch the calves and the toes and lie down again.

Finding Your Love Muscle

In order to gauge your love muscle's condition you will also need to touch it from inside your vagina. Exploring your anatomy may bring up some conditioned negative feelings for you. Some old dos and don'ts may dance across your mind. Let them go. I am not asking you to rush. Set the time up for yourself. The idea behind creating orgasm is not only exercise and the firmness, but the retention of the sensual atmosphere. And now it is an actual atmosphere you have created, in which you continue to feel sensual and know it is all right. Your exercises may be done in a variety of settings, but they will always call up the feelings you are establishing now. So prepare once again for pleasure and safety, and enter your real sensual room.

Take a hand mirror with you, and lie down in your safe room, resting naked. Do your breathing exercise, and check each body part for tension. Let your hand rest easily between your legs. Feel the mons veneris, or Mountain of Venus, and the curly, wiry, or silky hair and the pad of protective fat on it that covers the pubic bone. Place your hand over the outer part of the vagina, the vulva. Holding up your mirror between your legs, look at your vulva. Check the parts you can see against those in the diagram. Mirrors have a special value here. Just as dancers use mirrors to make the essential connection between what they are doing with a muscle and what it looks like, you can see how your muscles are moving in relation to your mental image of them.

Many women have never looked at their vaginas. Even some quite sexually active women have never looked. They feel they shouldn't, or that it's unnecessary, although they may have had several children. Be aware of what you are feeling. Some women have reported that their first reaction when looking at their vagina was nausea. Some felt shocked. They'd never seen it. The vulva (the external genitalia) may be lightly or more darkly colored and will have its unique arrangement of lips. When women in my workshops are shown pictures of different vaginas, they are astonished at the variety of shapes. They soon get over their shock at the unfamiliar and begin to realize the beauty and variety of their vagina and surrounding sensory tissues. In short, whatever your vagina and vulva look like, that is what they are *supposed* to look like.

Move your hand over the large outer lips around the vagina, the labia majora, and feel how they extend from your mons veneris downward, forming the outside borders of your vulva. These lips are delightfully sensitive. What are the shape and size of your lips?

Close your eyes and feel around the major lips. They lie close together in most women, appearing to keep the other parts of the vulva covered. Are your lips like that?

Look again. You are free to allow your feelings about sexual anatomy to surface. Stay with them. Float along with your imagination as you breathe

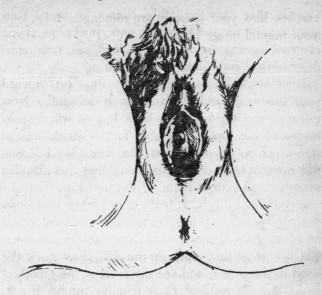

The female genitalia—the anatomy you love with

deeply and relax. Open the outer lips and begin to explore the minor ones, the labia minora. They are two thin folds of skin with an abundance of nerve endings and blood vessels. Often they are as sexually sensitive as the clitoris. Half of all women have larger minor lips than major lips. It is not unusual for one of the lips to be longer than the others. How do yours look in the mirror?

Below the vagina is the perineum, the space between the vagina and the anus. Touch the perineum. It is here that episiotomy cuts are made to widen the opening for childbirth. Do you have a scar visible?

Usually they fade until they cannot be seen. Your anus as you look at it may look pink, puckered. If you contract your love muscle you can see your anus draw inward and the perineum pull up.

Have you felt any vaginal lubrication yet? Spread your lips again and feel the tissue delicately. Now move to the top of your minor lips to where they merge at the top. There they form a single fold of skin which covers the clitoris, the clitoral hood. Touch the margin around the hood and feel the pleasant sensation. Do you remember the first time you discovered your clitoris? It is the only part of your body designed solely to bring you pleasure; it has no other function. As you move your finger gently around it feel if it is getting more prominent. Draw back the hood in the mirror and see the color of the top. Is it pink? Slightly redder? Does it move freely? If not, you might have clitoral adhesions, which constrict free movement of your clitoris and prevent its arousal.

Feel the texture of the soft membranes inside your vagina, and the thick feeling of the walls. The important thing is to let yourself experience whatever impressions, feelings, memories, or visual images arise now. This is an exercise in both pleasure and acceptance. Using creative visualization, imagine that instead of inhaling air through your nostrils, you are inhaling that lifegiving air into your vagina. Your vagina is that close and connected to you. It is bringing you life and breath. Here is the first entrance to the female anatomy, the anatomy that life springs from, the place of creation. Here you are building the pleasurable circuit of touching and receiving that touch. Relax deeply. In your mind, visualize a soft breath of air caressing your lips. It rushes past the outer lips and flows over your inner lips and into your vagina. This air is pure and revitalizing—it brings the promise of new energy and awareness. Breathe in and out as if with your vagina, and feel its connection to you, its health and beauty.

Feel with your finger now, approximately one finger joint inside the vagina. Here it feels soft and strong at the same time. This is the love muscle. To visualize your love muscle and make its location clear to you, place your fingers on your spinal column and move down to the last vertebra, your coccyx, to which one end of your love muscle is fastened. You may have spent a lifetime blissfully unaware of its existence, but if you've ever fallen on the coccyx, its location is indelible! Your love muscle is suspended between the coccyx and the pubic bone. If it hangs tautly, as it does in most young children, you have good muscle tone and strength; if it sags, you have a weak muscle. To your finger inside your vagina the muscle will feel ridged. Visualize it while you have your finger on it, and contract. Women who achieve good control often say they always visualize it in good condition, that is, in a straight line, when they contract it.

Is it hard to think of putting your fingers inside your vagina? I have no doubt that if you find your own body acceptable you will feel more alive and aware in life. This power can be channeled into a positive and fulfilling direction; it can enhance your desire to be a creative and successful woman. Taking risks like this gives you a higher level of self-esteem and lowers your anxiety about yourself. It frees up your energy.

With your finger feel the lubrication oozing from the walls of your vagina. If it feels uncomfortable, lubricate your finger with a gel and continue. Breathe easily. If you can reach more of your hand in, try to move your fingers until you feel a bump toward the back of the upper surface. That is the tip of your cervix. Some women want to view their cervixes for themselves, and there are medical devices that allow that. To some it looks pink and bulbous, like the head of a lubricated penis; to others it looks like a closed flower, or the end of a finger projecting into the vagina. In our mother's time, the idea that a woman might look at her own cervix was unthinkable. The latest research indicates that not only is the cervix pressure-sensitive, but it is also a source of pleasure. The uterus, too, into which the cervix leads, also seems to have a function other than childbearing. It has been recorded as an area that feels the contractions of orgasm.

With your hands touching your lower belly, visualize the uterus resting in your body like an upside-down pear, with the cervix as the neck. The skin of the pear is a web of muscles. Into the uterus come the tiny openings of the two Fallopian tubes down which your eggs travel. Did you know that your ovaries take turns releasing eggs? Now rest and place your hands once more over your vulva. On the upper surface of the vagina, if you wish to put your finger in to feel it, is a spot that researchers have recently discovered is the female equivalent of the male prostate. The evidence is that when it is stimulated some women are brought to ejaculate, sometimes with a squirt of fluid. It feels unpleasant when it is first stroked, but for some it yields great pleasure if the stroking is continued. This new erotic zone is called the Gräfenberg spot. It is located inside on the upper wall of the vagina, just under your bladder (press from above to find the bladder) and about an inch behind the pubic bone. When you first approach this spot with your hand, you will feel some tissue that feels just a little different from the surrounding tissue. As you stroke this spot, you first feel an intense, uncomfortable urge to urinate. But wait—if you continue stroking for a few seconds, the sensations become intensely erotic. The area will vary from the size of a dime to the size of a half dollar. As it is stimulated, the glandular tissue begins to swell, further demarking it from the surrounding tissue. The spot is now extremely sensitive and feelings of sexual arousal can take over if you would like them to. At this point most women notice that their vagina is quite wet—in fact for some the sensation is a familiar and unwelcome one—once again, they are afraid that they have urinated. That inhibiting thought has now been laid to rest. The flood of fluid released from the vagina or urinary meatus is actually ejaculate. Female ejaculate is clear. If, as you stimulate the spot, you keep a glass pressed below the vagina against the perineum you may find half a glass of clear fluid collected in the glass when you stop. The fluid flows out of your inverted urethra, but it does not contain urine. It is not yellow, and chemical tests reveal that it is primarily made up of acid phosphatase, the same chemical composition as the semen of men who have had vasectomies.

If you are one of the many women turned off and embarrassed about sex because you are sure that if you have an orgasm you will wet the bed, you may actually be one of the sensual women who have ejaculations. What has happened is that women have trained themselves to hold back the ejaculation and send it into the bladder, making it, we suspect, a retrograde ejaculation, and creating that urgent need to urinate after having an orgasm.

With these discoveries, it's time to venture back into that special room of your own. Relax, breathe deeply, stretch, and close your eyes. Open them, and reward yourself with praise.

Your Love Muscle's Condition Test

Once again, create privacy for yourself. This last assessment will take about ten minutes. Wash your hands, undress, and lie comfortably on the bed in your own space. Raise your knees and breathe to relax each part of your body. Gently insert a finger into your vaginal opening, using lubricant if necessary. Since your love muscle begins approximately one finger joint, or one or two inches, inside your vagina, penetration isn't a problem. If you are unsure about the depth to which to insert your finger, wrap soft tape around it at an inch and one-half, and you can feel when your finger is at the right depth.

First, feel the silky texture of the vaginal walls. Next, rub across the tissue holding your finger; it should feel ribbed, or corrugated. The general tissue will feel soft. You want to feel for the muscle, which will feel harder. If you rotate your finger, the ridges become more distinct. These muscular ridges are the love muscle. With your finger in this position continue to relax, breathing from the diaphragm; make sure you feel safe. Now contract your love muscle just as you did in the bathroom when you stopped the flow of urine. The ridges of the muscle will press against your finger and pull it upward toward your uterus. Relax your muscle and feel the pressure loosen. Do it again.

If the muscle is in good tone and strong it will draw against the fingers so tightly that in the extreme it can actually force your fingers out of your vagina. But don't worry if your muscle doesn't feel anything like that. It will. If it already has a viselike grip, you will certainly begin to gain stamina with exercise. What is important here is to identify the condition of your love muscle.

Tighten once more, and now try to release completely. Feel the muscles loosen completely, and let them go. Now tighten. Now you have tightening and releasing, the two basic skills of love muscle control.

Check the following table to find out your love muscle's condition.

LOVE MUSCLE CONDITION TEST

When I Squeeze Against My Finger I Feel	As I Rotate My Finger	As I Contract, My Finger	Condition Is
My muscle feels distinct, like rings of ribbing, or ribbed muscle tissue. It grips the finger.	The ribs become deeper and more distinct.	Is pulled up toward my uterus, or forcibly expelled or gripped	Good (Level One)
My muscle feels different from the surrounding tissue, but not very ribbed. It pulses when I contract	The ribs seem to remain the same; I have to push deeply.	Remains in the same position	Fair (Level Two)
My muscle feels soft. It does not press against my finger when I contract	The muscle feels as if the ribs are less distinct.	Can easily slip out	Poor (Level Three)

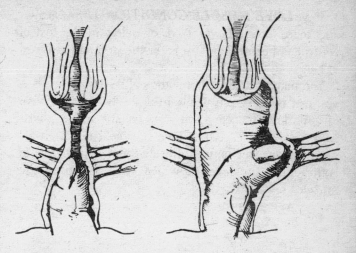

*My love muscle
is in good condition*   *A weak love muscle*

Setting Realistic Goals

If you are at Level One, "physically fit," but at Level Three, "poor," in either of the other tests, you enter at Level Two.

If you are at Level One in general fitness and score Level One or Two in both control and condition tests, you enter at Level One.

If you are in "fair," Level Two, physical condition and score Level Two or above in one or both tests, you enter at Level Two.

If you are "not active," or Level Three physical level, but score Level Two or above on one or both of the other tests, you enter at Level Two.

If you are "not active," Level Three physically, and score "fair," Level Two, or below in the test of control and condition, you enter the program at Level Three.

You may be at any combination of the above levels—you can be very physically fit and have poor control of your love muscle. You may be not active physically but have excellent love muscle control. It all depends on your natural muscle tone, your habits of contracting, the level at which you have used the muscle.

CHAPTER 4

Creating and Controlling Orgasm

The saying goes that knowledge is power. Surprisingly, the same idea applies to having an orgasm. Knowledge of what your orgasm is and what creates it actually makes it easier for you to come, not harder. It gives you the power to come when you want to. Does it sound impossible to "put an orgasm back together" once you have analyzed it? After all, when you're having an orgasm, you're not thinking. It seems either straightforward and mechanical, or so mysterious that it could never be "broken down" into separate parts.

But that's just what I'll do in this chapter. I'm going to examine the elements that make up orgasm. Science has a great deal more to say about it than was previously known. But you're also going to tease it and coax it, because playing with your orgasm is an art. Here you can not only create orgasm but become expert at sexuality. Far from getting in your way, these processes will assure you orgasm—and a lifetime of better health. And they are fun. Love muscle exercises make your orgasm longer and more intense! By the end of this chapter you'll know the art of both creating and controlling your orgasm, the secrets of real sexual expertise, and you will rise to a new level of sensuality.

What Is Orgasm?

Orgasm is the ultimate surrender to love. It is the physical expression of the union of the mind and body. At the moment of orgasm there is no struggle, no conflict, and no mind-body split. There is trust, integration, and the acceptance of pleasure. Orgasm is the line that connects all the points of our humanness to form a perfect circle; at that instant it is the center of the universe, of existence, of your life. That life is unfulfilled without the experience of joy that orgasm brings.

Ah, you say, you know that. Yet there has never before been a way to control orgasm completely, a way to come whenever and exactly when you want to. So the definition of orgasm must change. We are redefining it. The feelings inside you may be mysterious, they can never be anything but a connection to the infinite, but we now know how the mechanics of an orgasm work. I am going to show you exactly how to have control over orgasm. The old definitions that said having one was not controllable because orgasms are something someone else gives you no longer apply. What are we left with? Something even greater.

Orgasm is more than the release of muscle tension, muscle contractions, rapid breathing, and later relaxation; it is ecstasy. Followers of the Eastern religion of Tantra Yoga knew that orgasm connected them to the creative power in the universe. An orgasm is a connection to pure power, pure energy. In total letting go, you are flooded with you, connected to the force of creativity. Tantras nurtured and worshipped orgasm by gaining mastery over it and all their senses.

In this section are descriptions of how orgasms are triggered, how different bodies respond, and a set of exercises to prepare your love muscle for bringing on orgasm. Just as the fitness movement allowed almost half the American population who exercise regularly to gain command of their body's well-being and insure fitness for their heart, this chapter allows you to complete the job and pay technical attention to the other great, major muscle area of the body—just as vital to your health—the pelvic area.

I want to introduce the concept of being sexual all the time, just as you are fit (if involved in it) all the time. You are becoming physically and mentally conditioned to be orgasmic. Becoming sexually expert means knowing more about yourself.

How to Control Orgasm

Orgasm is a habit. That means that besides being a physical response it is a learned one. You acquire the habit of orgasm with certain specific stimulation.

What is a habit? A behavior that you want to repeat because it gives you *immediate gratification*. How strong your habit will be depends on what actions (your behaviors or environment) precede and follow that habit. These ideas are straight out of behavioral psychology. An orgasm is sandwiched between two sets of environmental influences—what happens before and what happens after. To get the habit of orgasm, and reinforce it, two series of steps are needed. The first is to become exactly aware of what you do. You notice and observe your own behavior before and after—during you're too busy! The second step is to use all your awareness to repeat or change your pattern, and practice the habit. Together the two steps amount to orgasm control. I'm going to cover them in depth.

Step 1: Awareness

1. Become aware when your body is feeling aroused.
2. Notice what turns you on in your everyday environment.
3. Observe your exact environment at the moment of sexual arousal.

4. Know when your love muscle is clenching and how to clench it. Be prepared by doing love muscle exercises.
5. Through creative visualization bond your turn-ons to the act of contracting your love muscle.

Step 2: Self-Reinforcing

1. Practice masturbating.
2. Do love muscle exercises.

How to Create Orgasm

What are the elements that create orgasm itself?

1. Relaxation. The habit that best creates orgasm is the one of relaxing. To that end you create a sensual atmosphere in which to relax. That's the reason we did the sensual room of your own. The other aspect of relaxing, of course, is to have easy acceptance of your own body, as discussed in chapter 2, "Preparation for Orgasm."
2. Your love muscle engorged with blood from clenching. That's the feeling of "hot." The clenching will by then be involuntary, but it is based on your regular love muscle exercises. The vaginal walls also tighten and narrow from the clenching, which is the natural position of a strong muscle. That brings the pleasure pressure receptors closer to stimulation.

3. Your mind and body bonded to "turn-ons"—your sexual images. Part of knowing your body is finding out what your turn-ons are. Bonding comes from your expectation of pleasure from being aroused, a habit.

4. Knowing all the rungs on the ladder, all the steps of your pleasure to orgasm, from masturbation.

Just doing your love muscle exercises alone will give you orgasm with stimulation. The other elements, the habit of orgasm, add reliability and beauty to your orgasm. To create orgasm, you must yield to yourself. To become a master you must bend to these elements, respond to what your body tells you.

Those who would conquer must yield; and those who conquer do so because they yield.

Lao-Tzu

Why Create and Control Your Own Orgasm?

Women often feel powerless in relationships with partners because they are dependent on their partners to give them an orgasm. It puts them in a one-down position. When you own your own orgasm, you know you can come. You are equal. With these exercises, you can, perhaps for the first time, be orgasmic when you want to with a partner. That's a beautiful thing—a miracle to have an orgasm when you want it with your love, with a man inside you. Here, for the first time, is a program that makes that possible.

Owning your orgasm gives you a sense of power. Women interested in becoming sexual experts have a high opinion of themselves. That's because they *are* doing something important. If you as a woman are involved in life as an autonomous human being, it makes you a delight to others, but you are still free to act from choice, not from other people's expectations. This sexual liberation gives you control of your life from the most primitive level.

If you are a woman stuck in the morass of basing your existence on a man, owning your own sexuality is a basic step in figuring out who you are. Studies show that when a woman has orgasms she is powerful; orgasms give us confidence that we are okay sexually. And that carries over into the world. We all need this kind of confidence. It gives women power as people, and with power come rights and a feeling of deserving the respect of others.

Expanding Your Sexuality: A Wider Look at Orgasm

What makes people come? It's important for you to know the many different ways in which people come, so that you can expand your own sexual repertoire. Once the basic response is there you can pick and choose what you want. If you have never come, one reason may be that you have simply not had any models to go by. On the following chart pages are listed many models, *a myriad of orgasms*. You can think through what you'd like.

Another reason for this list is that as orgasm is a habit, it's important to be aware of what you do or would like to do *before* having an orgasm.

You have already listed most of the habits you'd like around your orgasm, first among them your safe, comfortable environment. In your mind and in reality, that is the room of your own. You are aware of everything in it; it makes you feel sensual. Next, you deliberately stimulate your senses, feeling the effect and becoming aware of your body. You awaken your senses of

Touch
Sound
Smell
Sight
Taste

The stimulation of these senses is involved in every orgasm. When you add a feeling of emotional well-being, a sense of self-esteem, and the people you choose as partners, the elements needed for orgasm are complete.

Following is a list of some of the infinite variety of stimulations that lead directly to orgasm.

TYPES OF ORGASMS

This is a list of the various types of orgasms women have experienced. Content is based on new sex laboratory findings, clients' self-reports, workshop responses, and personal experience.

As you read the list, place a check next to each type of orgasm that is part of your sexual repertoire. If you are preparing for your first orgasm, here are a series of examples.

Orgasm with intercourse and clitoral stimulation_____

Orgasm from clitoral stimulation_____ Manual_____
  Vibrator_____

Orgasm with labia majora stimulation_____

Orgasm with labia minora stimulation_____

Orgasm with entire vulva stimulation and no penetration_____

Orgasm with penetration only and no clitoral stimulation_____
  Penis_____ Dildo_____ Finger_____ Other_____

Orgasm with anal stimulation_____ Penis____ Manual_____ Vibrator_____ Other_____

Orgasm with oral stimulation to outer, inner lips, and clitoris_____

Orgasm with oral stimulation to anus_____

Orgasm with breast stimulation_____ Hands_____
  Mouth_____ Other (fur, sensuous object)_____

Orgasm with ear stimulation_____

Orgasm with fantasy only_____

Orgasm with water_____

Orgasm from laughing_____

Orgasm from sports_____

Orgasm from riding horses, motorcycles_____

Orgasm from excitement_____ Racing cars, taking risks, playing roulette_____ Pressure situations_____ Exams, etc._____

Orgasm from winning, triumph_____

Orgasm from happy, joyful emotions_____

TOUCH
Orgasm from fingertip massage_____ Other tactile stimulation only_____

SIGHT
Orgasm from seeing a beautiful view_____ Work of art_____ Flowers_____

Orgasm from colors_____

SMELL
Orgasm from perfume_____ Smell of flowers_____ Body smells_____

OTHER
Orgasm from erotic movies_____ Books_____ Magazines_____ With stimulation_____ Without stimulation_____

Orgasm from observing beauty in nature_____
 Art_____ Music_____ People_____

Orgasm from religious experience_____

Orgasm from thought_____

Orgasm with uterine stimulation_____

Orgasm with cervical stimulation_____

Orgasm with Gräfenberg spot stimulation_____ From
 inside the vagina_____ From external pressure
 above it on the abdomen_____

Orgasm with partner's ejaculation_____

Orgasm with your ejaculation_____

The Gräfenberg Spot

Several of the kinds of orgasm on the list involve
the Gräfenberg spot, the newest orgasm of sexuality,
just discovered, and the hottest new area of sexual
investigation: female ejaculation.

The Gräfenberg spot, an area of sensitivity inside
the vagina, which you located in chapter 3, has been
found to be a source of orgasm. You can stroke the
dime-size area on the upper wall of your vagina until
it grows and swells in size. Most experimental subjects report that when they first do that the feeling is
extremely uncomfortable. All subjects report that it
gives them an urge to urinate. It almost burns. But
then, as they continue to stimulate it, many report
feeling extremes of pleasure. Women describe the

orgasm (or multiple orgasms) they get with Gräfenberg spot stimulation as different from the grand orgasm that seems to involve both vulval and uterine contractions. Perry and Whipple were able to measure contractions in both the vagina and the cervix/uterus during women's orgasms, which had never been done before, but when the Gräfenberg spot was stimulated some of their subjects reported a difference in the site of the contractions, as if only the vagina were involved.

This bears out the contention that no one area leads to orgasm, not just the clitoris or the vagina. As many women felt before there was scientific evidence to back them up, orgasms come from any and all of these stimulations. The Gräfenberg spot adds one more.

Sex researchers have evidence that some women can now reach orgasm by pressing on the Gräfenberg spot from the outside. The technique is to press down on the area just above the pubic bone over the bladder. You can feel the bladder pressing down onto the spot. Some women report orgasm just from pressing down on the bladder alone with a stroking motion. To palpate the spot itself from above, you press deeply until you feel the spot is being stimulated. Then the most surprising effect will occur.

All stimulation of the Gräfenberg spot causes the release of "excessive" watery fluid. This is female ejaculation. It is perfectly normal. Perry and Whipple have recorded it on film. Many women with a strong love muscle have reported feeling excessively wet during and right after making love. That is the ejaculate brought on from stimulation of the Gräfen-berg spot. As you rub the spot from inside or out, you may feel the flood of ejaculate oozing out, just as though you were milking the gland. If you want to try it, place a glass against your anus as you lie down with your feet on the bed, and your knees raised. Palpate the gland to where it feels pleasurable. After a while check the glass. You will probably find an astonishing amount of clear, colorless fluid collected! Some women have so concentrated on holding back what they always believed was their urine at the time of orgasm, that we believe they send the ejaculate backward into the bladder, in a retrograde ejaculation. The other side is women who squirt the fluid out at the moment of orgasm, sometimes to a distance of over a foot! Love muscle exercises will increase your ability to use and enjoy the added sensations of this gland before and during orgasm.

The Inner Orgasm

Another overlooked point of stimulation that can lead to glorious orgasm is the highly sensitive perito-neal tissue. This tissue covers the uterus and the broad ligaments in the lower abdominal area. When the cervix moves during intercourse, this sensitive tissue responds with erotic feeling and facilitates orgasm. Most women describe this "inner O" as hap-pening only with deep penetration, way back in the vagina, above their Gräfenberg spot.

In a paper that questioned the clitoral model of orgasm, Dr. Carol Rinkleib Ellison cited several cases where women felt these intense internal orgasms. One woman described the difference between the Gräfenberg spot orgasm and the "inner O" as follows:

"When we first heard about the Gräfenberg spot my husband and I experimented. I've been orgasmic with intercourse as long as I can remember. I have a magic spot way back in my vagina that's wonderful when I'm turned on and really intense just before orgasm. I can masterbate to orgasm with just clitoral stimulation, too. The Gräfenberg spot felt like it was hooked up completely separate from either of those, and they seem separate from each other, too. The Gräfenberg spot stimulation was pleasurable but seemed weak—like I needed to practice with it more often and it would get more intense. After a while I wanted my clitoris or my 'magic spot' stimulated so I could have my orgasm."

And so it seems that as more and more sexologists objectively examine female sexuality the phrase, "How shall I orgasm? Let me count the ways," is a true, marvelous fact of our sexual life.

Look Ma, No Hands!

Surely the most remarkable thing about this wider look at orgasm is that it shows that women can and do have orgasms *without any genital touching whatever*. By this time the contention that orgasm comes only from clitoral stimulation should be shown to be a narrow and restricting view. How much richer to be able to come from any and all types of stimulations. That is a possibility for *you* if you choose, as you journey further into this book. Imagine an orgasm without any genital stimulation at all. That is the end product of a total acceptance of your sexuality. What a wonderful thing to be able to do!

How is it possible? Two elements are necessary. The first comes from sexual experts called surrogates, who are trained to teach lovemaking to clients with sexual problems. They consistently report experiencing orgasms from being caressed on nongenital areas such as breasts, ear lobes, necks, even knees. Some of them become so in touch with their sexuality that they become able to have orgasms at will, with no touching.

A key element of surrogate training is that surrogates learn to widen their definition of sex, as we are doing here. They spend a lot of time training themselves to experience their entire body, not just their genitals, as an erogenous zone. Their job is to show clients new ways to derive pleasure from their own bodies without focusing on their genital areas. They build on the existing range of the person's sensory awareness, and expand its limits. The approach creates new neurological pathways that are associated with pleasure, and they reinforce the positive psychological habits.

The second aspect of achieving "no hands" orgasms is that people who report them always concentrate on contracting their love muscle. They concentrate on coming, and they concentrate on clenching their muscle.

When I interviewed Cicely Green, one of the first women to take surrogate training, I asked, "When did you become aware of your ability to have an orgasm by contracting your muscle?"

"When I began my surrogate training, where Dr. Kegel's exercises were a mandatory thing and I began to do them. That's when I found out that if I really focused on them as I did them, that sometimes I had an orgasm while doing them. It doesn't seem to make any difference which you do, the main thing is to get the muscle in tone. I believe that the thing that trips my orgasm is the focus."

Physiologically, when the muscle is contracted it engorges with blood. Vascongestion is one phase of sexual arousal; in fact it creates the sexual tension that is released in orgasm.

I asked Cicely, "When you focus, exactly what are you focusing on?"

"I do visualizations. My mind is on pictures, sounds. What I visualize is the blood from various parts of my body flowing relentlessly, crawling toward this one place. I happen to visualize it as the mons. As I see that happening, the blood does come in, and I am conscious of a growing warmth and pressure and that's the thing that builds up the tension until I have an orgasm.

"It doesn't necessarily happen when I'm doing the exercises in my regular daily practice. I don't focus on it as much. It happens when I use the exercises to stop boredom. For example, when I'm sitting in a boring meeting, or going to lectures, or seminars, sometimes they're two or three days long, and you're sitting eight hours a day. The material might be boring, and there is little stimulation. One of the ways I pass the time or keep alert is to do my exercises and really focus on them. Then I can willfully do the contractions, and then, at a point, I have stopped willfully doing the contractions, and I let them take off on their own."

Can it be done at will? "To bring back the mechanism, I can use fantasy. We are our own biofeedback machines. By focusing on specific details we can replay anything in our experience. I do not look at what my general overall feeling was about, at all. Instead, I recall specifics, the exact colors, the shapes, the sounds, the textures, the odors, each individually.

"The minute I leave myself open to remembering in detail, it brings back the whole bunch of other memories of that event, as well as of the sensory input, and together they trip my orgasm as if it's happening now for the first time."

Cicely's report is that of someone who is totally focused on her sexuality for professional reasons. The climate of being constantly involved with sex has something to do with it too. But her experiences are not just for the expert. Sex lab studies validate that many women have had orgasms from smells, colors, sounds, and fantasy. Once you have the ability to orgasm, it will be possible for you to put that ability under your conscious control.

Do You Have Orgasms?

Historically, women's orgasms have been owned by somebody else. In our time they were defined as something a man gave you. For most of history, however, the value systems that controlled sexual behavior simply left out woman's orgasms altogether.

Religion played its part in controlling the lustful side of man, and therefore women. But the lust was all male. Even so, people wondered, Why did God give us this body, capable of such exquisite pleasure? If we believe the sexual instinct is wrong, then why did God make us? Did he make a tragic mistake?

I believe that sex is necessary, and so is its pleasure.

During the time women weren't even supposed to be turned on, they certainly weren't free to masturbate. Victorian psychologists called masturbation "self-abuse"; they said it would make you crazy. Of course, they were speaking to men. Women weren't even allowed to *go* crazy from masturbation, because they didn't do it.

That was unfortunate for many generations of women, because what science discovered was that you learn to have an orgasm by masturbating. When The Pill and scientific study liberalized sex, women felt pressured to experiment widely, and masturbation was advocated.

But there was a catch to that, too. Even with all the sexual freedom, many women have still had no orgasm, or can't rely on having one. The problem was that they were being told that they should be able to come with *everybody*. No one can do that. Being promiscuous was not the answer. I know because they come to my workshops. What they wanted was to learn from the experts how to have an orgasm in a systematic way. They learned from me and each other what is now in this book: how to have an intense and open connection to your own and your partner's pleasure. To have an orgasm, you need to trust yourself first, to hear what your body is saying to you, and act to get it. That is also what you do with your partner.

Do you have orgasms? Yes, it's very important that everyone have orgasms. Do you want to open this door now? It means change. It means risk-taking and having power. The power is that your connection to sexuality is not static. Sexual expression is not limited to orgasm—it can be taken to the highest levels. You can move with it into a creative level. You can have orgasms twenty times a day, if you want to, but that's not the point.

The point is that you are already becoming your own best sexual expert. Whatever your level, by now you are already becoming developed and advanced. With heightened sensitivity to your own sexuality, you will certainly enter a new dimension.

The Aphrodisiac of Risk

Why is risk a turn-on, and why risk to orgasm? Risk-taking is Douglas Fairbanks, Jr., and buckling your swash. It's supposed to be the province of men. Except it isn't anymore. Most women now have to take risks all the time to survive. These are risks having to do with the use of power.

Feeling easy with risk makes it easier to have an orgasm. Risk is an aphrodisiac, with a role in the creation and control of orgasm.

The reward of risk-taking is an increase in power. The concept has wide implications. Business seminars that prepare women for management regularly deal with the problems they will face in the male world of business and the professions. For example, graduates of the highly regarded Boston's Simmons College for women hold some of the top spots in management. Courses there leading to the M.B.A. degree spend about half their time familiarizing women with the methods and mores of a male atmosphere— the manipulation of power and risk-taking, both prime power-seeking behaviors. Women who want an executive career practice risk-taking in their courses because it is a prerequisite for success in the male system of things—*and women have never learned it*.

When you take the risk and have the mental responsibility for your orgasm, you are free to leave hidden struggles over power issues out of sexuality.

You may be overwhelmed with bills and juggling

schedules, you may be coping with the traditional pressures at work and at home, but with all that you have a much greater responsibility for control of your own life. Being familiar with risk-taking is another kind of security.

You can feel safe with the amount of risk here. The pressure is removed. We hope that it becomes less of a risk to be sexual. Feminism gave many women their first experience of an external support system. It allowed many to gain the confidence and esteem to expand their power base. I encourage you also. Pleasure *is* power, because it *gives you* power. Because of that pleasure can seem scary.

What is the risk in this program? Learning something new. *If you are orgasmic*, you will intensify your orgasm and prolong it. You have never done *this* program before, because it's never been around until now. That's the sense of excitement, in these pages, that I invite you to turn into sexual pleasure.

Risk-taking is having this program and doing it, and doing the homework—which I can only call funwork, because it gives pleasure. All you risk is becoming your own best expert. This is the first time in history we have had that option.

Your Love Muscle Exercises

I hope that right this minute you are clenching your love muscle and feeling the excitement of learning how to create and control your orgasm. Here is a systematic program to help you.

There are three basic types of love muscle exercises.

1. The slow and sustained grip
2. The pulse
3. The push and pull

Take a few moments to get a clear picture of each.

The Slow and Sustained Grip

This exercise, considered by many experts as the most effective, squeezes and holds your love muscle in a prolonged contraction, beginning with three seconds and then gradually increasing the time of the contraction to a ten-second sustained hold. At the very end of the contraction, squeeze once rapidly, harder and deeper, then release.

Count: one, two, three, four, five (and more), gripping, then grip hard, up to the top. Holding and gripping builds endurance and strength by gradually stressing the muscle to maintain a contracted position. This in turn lengthens and narrows the vaginal walls, bringing them closer together.

Between each contraction relax the muscle *completely*. Complete relaxation is critical to improving endurance, because it allows the muscle to rest and gain more from subsequent contractions. Relaxing the muscle completely between contractions gives greater and quicker results.

The Pulse

In this exercise you rapidly contract and release your muscle, in time to a fast beat. One good rhythm to use is the beat of your heart. Feel the pulse beat. How many times does it beat per minute? Begin by clenching on every other beat. If this is too difficult, space the intervals between clenches until you can easily distinguish when the muscle is relaxing and when it is contracting. Count the number of beats between contractions. Your goal is to cut down the beats between the contractions. The aim of this exercise is to build endurance, until you can clench at every beat. In my experience it's this exercise that is most effective in triggering orgasm.

Soon, practice will pay off and you will have increased voluntary control over your love muscle as well as new sexual sensations in your pelvis.

Because it is so easily done, this exercise is also the one I regularly recommend for practice outside your home as you go on with the daily business of your life.

The Push and Pull

This exercise works as a general toner for the entire pelvis, since it raises the pelvic floor and uses the muscles in the stomach and abdominal wall in addition to the love muscle. It's a good one to do in the morning in bed. It also stimulates vaginal lubrication and circulation in the vaginal and uterine muscles and therefore is highly recommended prior to sexual activity, particularly intercourse.

This exercise has three parts, each lasting for five seconds. I've saved it for last because it is a bit more complex, yet it is as rewarding as the rest.

The first step is to breathe deeply while you contract the love muscle and for two seconds continuously pull up the floor of the pelvis as if you had a tampon inside your vaginal canal. You can feel the walls of your vagina surrounding it. Now contract against it and make a motion as if you wanted to suck the tampon higher up. (I am not suggesting you do this with an actual tampon, because of the danger of toxic shock syndrome). Then, hold the pulled-in position for at least two seconds (you'll gradually build up to five), keeping the imagined tampon high inside the vagina. You can also imagine it is water that you want to keep in and draw up high.

The last step is to push out or bear down in a continuous two-second motion, as if you were forcing the tampon out of your vagina. If you do use tampons, you can practice this motion with the tampon in and see if you can expel it with your vaginal muscles.

Breathe out. As you relax after bearing down, give your love muscle one good final squeeze up to its tightest clench.

Your Exercise Schedule

Now that you know the basic exercises, the following chart gives you the schedule of exercises to follow, according to your level. These guidelines are designed to prevent you from overfatiguing the muscle or getting discouraged at how long you can exercise at first. If you find you can advance faster, however, do so. There isn't any such thing as too much love muscle exercise once you feel comfortable doing it.

Your schedule is based on two elements of athletic theory: "repeats" and "interval training." Repeats are how many times you do something in a row, which stresses the muscle and forces endurance. Intervals are a pattern of how many sets you do with how much rest in between, which builds up your cardiovascular capacity. Your muscle will work best if you work it in sets, gradually building up to harder, faster ones, with rest breaks in between. If you've ever seen a pool full of competitive swimmers doing a workout, swimming up and down to some mysterious pattern, you'll note that they stop every now and then to check their pulses and look at the huge clock that sits on the side of every competitive pool. They are following a prearranged schedule of intervals and repeats. The same athletic theory, responsible for most of the advances in today's athletics, applies to your program.

With your love muscle exercises the aim is to slightly stress the muscle on a regular basis, gradually increasing the stress. You increase the amount of work your muscle must do, just like a runner building up endurance. That makes it demand more oxygen, build up a better vascular system, and gain muscle tone.

The following charts incorporate this technical approach, but you don't need to know the theory; the charts are very simple to follow for each level. The charts are keyed to your level. If you follow them faithfully, you will have a lifetime of joy and health.

This program takes six weeks.

Exercise can be pleasurable. Many of us, as women, were not raised on exercise. For most of us, exercise means work, not pleasure. It is particularly disassociated from anything sexual. And I won't lie to you: this program does take work.

Getting started is always the hardest part of building a new habit. If you have particular trouble with exercise, give yourself a special reward after you have done the first week of exercise.

If you are already accustomed and committed to exercise, beginning and mastering this program will give you great pleasure. You already know the joy that complete body fitness brings. Like all good exercise, love muscle exercise releases endorphins, a chemical compound that acts as a natural analgesic.

Give yourself two weeks of practicing your program before you expect the first signs of the control that you will later achieve. It takes time for muscle control. But rest assured that the exercise will begin to intensify sexual pleasure almost immediately.

LEVEL THREE

First Week

Day 1   Slow and sustained grip
    10 minutes in A.M.   10 minutes in P.M.
Day 2   Pulse
    10 minutes in A.M.   10 minutes in P.M.
Day 3   Push and pull/pulse
Alternate 5 minutes each
    10 minutes in A.M.   10 minutes in P.M.
Day 4   Slow and sustained grip/pulse
Alternate 5 minutes each
    10 minutes in A.M.   10 minutes in P.M.
Day 5   Slow and sustained grip
    10 minutes in A.M.   10 minutes in P.M.
Day 6   Pulse/slow and sustained grip
    10 minutes in A.M.   10 minutes in P.M.
Day 7   Slow and sustained grip
    10 minutes in A.M.   10 minutes in P.M.

LEVEL THREE

Second Week

Stick with it.

Day 1	Slow and sustained grip
	10 minutes A.M. 10 in P.M.
Day 2	Pulse
	10 minutes A.M. 10 in P.M.
Day 3	Push and pull/pulse
	10 minutes A.M. 10 in P.M.
Day 4	Pulse
	15 minutes A.M. 10 in P.M.
Day 5	Rest
Day 6	Slow and sustained grip
	15 minutes A.M. 10 in P.M.
Day 7	Pulse/push and pull/slow and sustained grip
	Alternate 5 minutes each
	15 minutes A.M. 10 in P.M.

LEVEL THREE

Third Week

If you have previously been preorgasmic, or have been having trouble achieving orgasm, you may find that condition has happily changed during this week.

Day 1   Slow and sustained grip
          15 minutes A.M.   10 in P.M.
Day 2   Pulse
          15 minutes A.M.   15 in P.M.
Day 3   Push and pull/pulse
          15 minutes A.M.   15 in P.M.
Day 4   Slow and sustained grip/pulse
          15 minutes A.M.   15 in P.M.
Day 5   Slow and sustained grip/pulse
          20 minutes A.M.   15 in P.M.
Day 6   Pulse/push and pull
          15 minutes A.M.   15 in P.M.
Day 7   Slow and sustained grip/pulse
          20 minutes A.M.   20 in P.M.

LEVEL THREE

Fourth Week

Congratulations, your muscle is as strong now as many of those who started at higher levels. Twenty minutes twice a day, now that's not bad. It's also your goal in terms of time. Now that you have become relatively expert, however, it's time to start counting strokes in terms of the number of clenches per exercise session. Now you are also expert enough to make an effort to relax the muscles completely between each clench.

Day 1   Slow and sustained grip
     20 minutes A.M. 5 in midafternoon   20 in P.M.
          Strokes done: 150

Day 2   Pulse
     20 minutes A.M. 5 in midafternoon   20 in P.M.
          Strokes done: 200 or more

Day 3   Push and pull/pulse
     20 minutes A.M. 10 in midafternoon 20 in P.M.
          Strokes done: 100

Day 4   Slow and sustained grip/pulse
     20 minutes A.M. 10 in midafternoon 20 in P.M.
          Strokes done: 150

Day 5   Slow and sustained grip/pulse
     20 minutes A.M. 10 in midafternoon 20 in P.M.
          Strokes done: 200

Day 6   Slow and sustained grip/push and pull
     20 minutes A.M. 10 in midafternoon 20 in P.M.
          Strokes done: 150

Day 7   Slow and sustained grip/pulse/push and pull
     20 minutes A.M. 15 in midafternoon 20 in P.M.
          Strokes done: 200

LEVEL THREE

Fifth and Sixth Weeks

You have come the farthest, and you have shown the greatest perseverence.

Fifth Week: Keep the 20 minutes A.M./10 midafternoon/20 minutes P.M. schedule. Alternate the exercises. Work on relaxing completely between each stroke and then pulling up as quickly as possible. Your goal: 300 strokes (clenches) per day.

Sixth Week: 20 minutes A.M./20 minutes P.M.

Alternate the exercises, increasing your speed and strength of contractions. Enjoy the sensual aspects of what you have accomplished. Work up to: 300 strokes a day.

This is also your lifetime maintenance schedule, for orgasm and pelvic health.

LEVEL TWO

First Week

Day 1   Slow and sustained grip
    5 minutes A.M.   5 in P.M.
Day 2   Pulse
    5 minutes A.M.   5 in P.M.
Day 3   Push and Pull
    5 minutes A.M.   5 in P.M.
Day 4   Slow and sustained grip
    10 minutes A.M.   5 in P.M.
Day 5   Slow and sustained grip/pulse
    Alternate 5 minutes each
    10 minutes A.M.   10 in P.M.
Day 6   Push and pull/pulse
    10 minutes A.M.   10 in P.M.
Day 7   Slow and sustained grip/pulse
    10 minutes A.M.   10 in P.M.

LEVEL TWO

Second Week

Day 1   Slow and sustained grip
            10 minutes A.M.   10 in P.M.
    Begin to try to get complete relaxation of the muscle
    between grips.
Day 2   Pulse/slow and sustained grip
            10 minutes A.M.   10 in P.M.
Day 3   Pulse/slow and sustained grip
            10 minutes A.M.   10 in P.M.
Day 4   Push and pull
            10 minutes A.M.   5 in P.M.
Day 5   Rest
Day 6   Slow and sustained grip/pulse
            10 minutes A.M.   10 in P.M.
Day 7   Slow and sustained grip/pulse/push and pull
            10 minutes A.M.   10 in P.M.

LEVEL TWO

Third Week

Day 1   Slow and sustained grip
   10 minutes A.M.   10 in P.M.
Day 2   Pulse/slow and sustained grip
   15 minutes A.M.   15 in P.M.
Day 3   Slow and sustained grip/push and pull
   15 minutes A.M.   15 in P.M.
Day 4   Pulse
   15 minutes A.M.   15 in P.M.
Day 5   Slow and sustained grip/pulse
   15 minutes A.M.   15 in P.M.
Day 6   Pulse/push and pull
   15 minutes A.M.   15 in P.M.
Day 7   Pulse/slow and sustained grip
   20 minutes A.M.   15 in P.M.

LEVEL TWO

Fourth Week

You are becoming quite adept and strong now. Try to concentrate on the differences of feeling between the different exercises, and what areas of the vagina feel this most. Practice breathing more deeply. I hope you are enjoying the increased feelings of sensuality. Your muscle is getting enough of a workout now to do better with a brief rest during each session. Put in a one-minute rest, or interval, where indicated.

Day 1	Slow and sustained grip	
	15 minutes A.M.	20 in P.M.
Day 2	Pulse	
	20 minutes A.M. (in two	20 in P.M.,
	segments, 3-minute break)	3-minute break
Day 3	Slow and sustained grip	
	20 minutes A.M.,	20 in P.M.,
	2-minute break	2-minute break
Day 4	Pulse/slow and sustained grip	
	20 minutes A.M.,	20 in P.M.,
	2-minute break	2-minute break
Day 5	Push and pull/pulse	
	20 minutes A.M.,	20 in P.M.,
	1-minute break	1-minute break
Day 6	Slow and sustained grip	
	20 minutes A.M.,	20 in P.M.,
	1-minute break	1-minute break
Day 7	Pulse/slow and sustained grip/push and pull	
	20 minutes A.M.,	20 in P.M.,
	1-minute break	1-minute break

LEVEL TWO

Fifth and Sixth Weeks

Now you have reached so advanced a level that you can probably pulse quite fast. Work on relaxing the muscle completely between each of the strokes, for example, in the slow and sustained grip. You will be doing a twenty-minute session with two segments (called repeats) with a one-minute break in between (the interval).

Fifth Week: Count your strokes in each segment. Work up to 150 clenches. Do 20 minutes A.M., 1-minute break and 20 minutes P.M., 1-minute break.

Alternate your exercises at will.

Sixth Week: Count your strokes. Your goal is 300 strokes and relaxings per day. Maintenance is 20 minutes A.M. and 20 minutes P.M., all exercises, 1 minute breaks, and a goal each day of 300 strokes.

Congratulations. You're an expert now.

LEVEL ONE

First Week

Are we going to have fun! There's nothing like it—these exercises feel wonderful. It will be wonderful for you to master another area of your body, and one that is so important. You will very soon be doing the thrusting and gripping patterns in "Exercise for the Advanced." But let's awaken those muscles first.

Day 1	Slow and sustained grip	
	10 minutes A.M.	5 in P.M.
Day 2	Slow and sustained grip	
	10 minutes A.M.	10 in P.M.
Day 3	Pulse	
	10 minutes A.M.	10 in P.M.
Day 4	Push and pull	
	5 minutes A.M.	5 in P.M.
Day 5	Slow and sustained grip/pulse	
	Alternate them	
	10 minutes A.M.	10 in P.M.
Day 6	Slow and sustained grip/pulse	
	10 minutes A.M.	10 in P.M.
Day 7	Push and pull/pulse	
	10 minutes A.M.	10 in P.M.

LEVEL ONE

Second Week

You are already aware of the necessity of relaxing a muscle after you have been using it for a while. There are two kinds of relaxation to isolate in the use of the love muscle. The first is totally relaxing *between* each clench. The second is a full recuperation time between repeats, as indicated. This gives the muscle time to build mass. You will also be building an increased blood supply and regenerating or causing the proliferation of nerve endings in this wonderful muscle.

Day 1	Slow and sustained grip	
	Relax muscle between each grip	
	10 minutes A.M.	10 in P.M.
Day 2	Pulse/slow and sustained grip	
	15 minutes A.M.	10 in P.M.
Day 3	Push and pull/pulse	
	15 minutes A.M.	15 in P.M.
Day 4	Pulse/push and pull	
	15 minutes A.M.	15 in P.M.
Day 5	Rest	
Day 6	Push and pull/pulse/slow and sustained grip	
	15 minutes A.M.	15 in P.M.
Day 7	Slow and sustained grip	
	15 minutes A.M.,	15 in P.M.,
	1-minute break	1-minute break

LEVEL ONE

Third Week

You must be feeling quite fit all over. I hope you are still taking the time to do your usual fitness routines. In chapter 7, I tell how to combine these exercises with several sorts of fitness activities, such as running and aerobic dance (including warmups), which you may want to look at. I hope the sexual benefits of these exercises have now become delightful.

Day 1	Slow and sustained grip
	10 minutes A.M. 5 in midafternoon 10 in P.M.
Day 2	Pulse/slow and sustained grip
	10 minutes A.M. 5 in midafternoon 10 in P.M.
Day 3	Pulse/push and pull
	15 minutes A.M. 15 in P.M.
Day 4	Slow and sustained grip/pulse
	20 minutes A.M. 20 in P.M.
Day 5	Slow and sustained grip/push and pull
	10 minutes A.M. 10 in midafternoon 10 in P.M.
Day 6	Pulse/slow and sustained grip
	20 minutes A.M. 20 in P.M.
Day 7	Pulse/slow and sustained grip
	20 minutes A.M., 20 in P.M.,
	1-minute break 1-minute break

LEVEL ONE

Fourth Week

Can you separate which part of the vagina you are clenching? Do you like to pulse in the middle, but do the slow and sustained grip as high as possible? Have you experienced any stimulation of the Gräfenberg spot during the push and pull? It is likely that with your strong muscle, which may have been in excellent shape from birth, you may feel some stimulation of this spot, which is all to the good.

Day 1	Slow and sustained grip/push and pull	
	20 minutes A.M.,	20 in P.M.,
	1-minute break	1-minute break
Day 2	Slow and sustained grip/push and pull	
	20 minutes A.M.,	20 in P.M.,
	1-minute break	1-minute break

You are advanced enough now to begin counting your strokes. Each time you clench, count 1. Remember to relax completely between clenches, and work on speed with control.

Day 3	Pulse	
	20 minutes A.M.,	20 in P.M.,
	1-minute break	1-minute break
		150 strokes
Day 4	Slow and sustained grip	
	20 minutes A.M.,	20 in P.M.,
	1-minute break	1-minute break
		150 strokes

Day 5   Push and pull/pulse
    20 minutes A.M.,   20 in P.M.,
    1-minute break   1-minute break
                                         150 strokes
Day 6   Slow and sustained grip
    20 minutes A.M.,   20 in P.M.,
    1-minute break   1-minute break
                                         150 strokes
Day 7   Slow and sustained grip/pulse/push and pull
    20 minutes A.M.,   20 in P.M.,
    1-minute break   1-minute break
                                         200 strokes

LEVEL ONE

Fifth and Sixth Weeks

Now you are a virtuoso. Your expertise can extend to isolating a certain area of your vagina, or to alternating the different patterns at will, or to sustaining a contraction for upward of three minutes. Try it; see how many minutes you can hold for in a set of ten repeats in the slow and sustained grip. Shoot for three minutes.

Fifth Week: 20 minutes A.M.   20 in P.M.

Mix your exercises at will, remembering to relax after each contraction, but working up until each day's workout totals up to 300 strokes.

A delightful variation:

20 minutes in A.M., begin with slowest strokes. The slow and sustained grip for 5 minutes. Then speed up in the pulse for the next 5 minutes and take your 1-minute break. Then repeat that pattern for the next ten minutes.

20 minutes in P.M. Begin with slowest strokes for 10 minutes, then break for 1 minute. Then 5 minutes at moderate, slow and sustained grip, and finish with 5 minutes of the pulse at your fastest. This is the principle of sprints, and you can use it to build your muscle. Maintenance: 20 minutes A.M. 20 in P.M., 1-minute breaks, alternating exercises. Include two sessions with sprints each week. Your goal is 300 strokes a day for a lifetime.

The time indicated, even if it takes the longest possible time, is a small price to pay for the marvelous lift you will receive from even one session of exercise, and a lifetime of pelvic health and orgasm.

The time needed will be shorter if you do your exercises every day, longer if you do them, for example, three times a week.

Creating and controlling orgasm will take time. In all programs for creating orgasm, those women who practiced the most and most consistently were those who achieved orgasm. There was almost a one-to-one correlation. Only those who do take the time to go through the processes as they are outlined here will achieve full knowledge and love muscle control. The reason is that this is a program of establishing behavior patterns. Research tells us that anything you do before you have sex will influence your response. In these pages I create new patterns to create a new response.

Your Progress Reports

After the first week you are ready to begin keeping a record of your progress in your journal. (As with any exercise you do, remember to breathe. That muscle needs oxygen. You may even find your posture improving as your lungs gasp for more oxygen.)

Your level of control will show improvement not only in your orgasm but also in how long you can comfortably exercise during any one session.

If you want to keep a running check, you can keep a love muscle journal record of your exercise times and reps.

Love Muscle Journal Entry
Love muscle development and exercise record

Time started session	Time completed	Total Time	Total for day	Number of 5-minute sets	Done while traveling, working, etc.	Goal today

How to Tell If You Are Improving

You are. Right now, clenching your muscle, you are improving. It's a no-lose situation—you gain *just* thinking about it! The more you clench, whether for two minutes or just casually all day, the stronger and more filled with blood your muscle will become. If real expertise is your goal, and you are following the schedule carefully, your level of control will show improvement very rapidly. With all control over your love muscle you will experience increased "orgasmic return," in other words, depending upon your body, you will begin to experience orgasm more easily.

After the first week of exercise, notice, if you have kept a journal record, how long you can now comfortably continue with your exercises in any one session. That is a timetable measure of your improvement. You'll be amazed at how rapidly this wonderful muscle "leaps" at the chance to get strong and alive. Dr. Kegel, way back when, reported being amazed that even with their muscle in its weakest, most unused condition, even after surgery, women could improve in as little as three weeks! He remarked that he knew of no other muscle system in the body so equipped to repair itself.

After one month of love muscle awareness and as much clenching as you have been able to pursue, reassess your progress in the light of your goals. Your goals may be

1. Orgasm
2. To enhance and prolong orgasm
3. Narrowing of the vaginal walls
4. Prevention and cure of urinary stress incontinence (and a variety of other health problems; see chapter 7)
5. Mastery of the refinements of sexual expertise

You may have already reached several goals. For general level, go back to chapter 3 and check your love muscle control and condition tests. You will find an astonishing improvement in your muscle strength and tone. Stopping your urine flow when you go to the bathroom is always available to you as a quick check to see if your muscle is in good condition. This program is a daily thing, a part of your life, and a pleasant, self-perpetuating one.

What if your goals went further, past health and strength? What if you're exercising for sexual expertise? There have been revolutions in the study of sex you will want to be informed about. As Zorba the Greek said, "Ah, my friend, I have so much to tell you."

The Habit of Orgasm

The habit of orgasm is formed in two steps. The first is awareness of the stimulus that precedes the orgasm, how and when you get turned on; the second is masturbation.

In this section you will get the power to take your love muscle exercises all the way to orgasm.

Sex research shows that arousal is expressed by both conscious and unconscious contractions of the love muscle. Women automatically contract the muscle when they see something that excites them. Trouble is, most women aren't tuned in to acknowledge these erotic sensations. Remember the "dead zone" phenomenon, the area from waist to thighs that is devoid of feeling in many women? And don't forget the cultural taboos that program women to ignore their sexuality as a means of controlling their destiny. We learn to turn off! Now it's time to learn to turn on. For a start, when you do your love muscle exercises, you'll be turned on anyway—blood engorges the muscle, tensions increases, and you've reached the first stage of human sexual response, excitement.

If you feel afraid of losing control you can deal with this by setting limits. You can govern how much you do until you feel comfortable with the sensations. If you feel as if you are losing control, cool out. Set smaller steps for yourself. But, if the situation is right, sink into the feeling and take it to the limit.

To put the important stimuli that precede your orgasm under your control, here is a list of turn-ons.

WHAT AROUSES YOU?

In the last chapter you recorded two things that excited you when you clenched your love muscle. If you didn't clench to those images, think of two now. There is no rush about this, take a day or two if you want, and just go around looking at turn-ons and see when your muscle clenches.

If you did write down two, what were they? _____

_____

How often did you contract your love muscle to this turn-on?_____

What do you turn on to? Any of the following?

PEOPLE

Opposite sex	Back turned
Same sex	Moving
Attractive	In fantasy
Unattractive	In movies
In the flesh	On TV
Half-dressed	In magazines
Fully dressed	Erotic
Smiling	Pornographic
Unsmiling	Fashion
Facing you	Art
Half-turned	Photography

LOOKS

Lean	Short
Dark	Neat
Heavy	Clean
Thick	Fair
Tall	

MOVEMENTS

Quick	Artistic
Energetic	Athletic
Graceful	Slow

VOICES

Soft	Whispering
Deep	Singing

| Low | Laughing |
| Steady | Confident |

HANDS

Hard	Small
Soft	Calloused
Artistic	Competent
Delicate	Touching
Big	Firm

ASPECTS OF THE BODY

Eyes	Ass
Hair	Feet
Smile	Ankles
Lips	Chests/breasts
Bones	Builds
Shoulders	Slender
Skin	Average
Hands	Muscular
Thighs	Large
Back	Fat

SCENTS

Perfumes	Sweat
Scent of a face	Cologne
After shave	Sweet Breath

OBJECTS

Paintings	Fabrics
Jewelry	Satin, brocade
Furs	

ANIMALS

Horses with rippling   Cats
  muscles

NATURAL OBJECTS

Water   Textures
Flowers   Views
Light and color

MY ACTIONS

Bathing   Buying things
Showering   Doing a sport
Undressing   Dancing
Putting on makeup   Swimming
Putting on stockings   Wearing certain clothing,
Walking naked   sportsy, low-cut

Hots and Bonds

To create the habit of orgasm you now bond one of your most exciting turn-ons with each of your love muscle exercises. The surest path to orgasm is to combine your exercises with the power of visualization. From now on, then, clench your muscle at an arousing stimulus. Choose one specific turn-on for each of the exercises. To form this habit strongly, notice all the details of this turn-on: color, sound, and form. It works best to have a distinct, separate turn-on for each exercise; it simplifies things. You've got a lot to think about, especially at first.

The following chart and pages will assist you in the bonding.

Love Muscle Exercise Bonding Chart

A JOURNAL ENTRY

Decide which turn-on you choose to associate with *each* love muscle exercise.

1. The slow and sustained grip   1._____
2. The pulse   2._____
3. The push and pull   3._____

Whenever you clench at a turn-on tell yourself you're great, because you are doing something great. That and your pleasure will give you an upward spiral of pleasure and reinforcement.

It's easy to start feeling there's something wrong with you if you walk around turned on all the time. But why not? Now that your exercises are bonded with a turn-on, you may feel turned on all the time, and that's good!

It means you're truly alive.

A New Look at Masturbation

This is a chapter about mastery. The fulfillment of the erotic process of owning your own orgasm is masturbating. Surprisingly enough, for something so pleasurable, masturbation has had a lot of bad press.

Masturbation teaches you how to have an orgasm. In all sex workshops it's an assigned homework for people who have never had an orgasm before. All the data confirm that orgasm is one of the most powerful reinforcers known to humankind. You can use it to reinforce itself, or your great feelings about yourself, or what you want to do in any area of your life. For example, in this case, be consciously aware of using your orgasm to reinforce your love muscle exercises. That's dynamite power.

Masturbating to orgasm, especially in the environment you have already created, combined with your love muscle patterns, is an excellent way to get in touch with yourself. Kinsey reported in 1953 that 94 percent of women reach orgasm 95 percent of the time with masturbation. Masters and Johnson reported in 1966 that orgasms with masturbation were more dependable and took a shorter time to reach than with a partner.

There's been another side to masturbation, the side in more recent sexual literature. Recently experts have swung full circle and extolled it—especially masturbation with clitoral stimulation—as the *only* way to reach orgasm. I want to drop all that. As we've seen, the ways to reach orgasm are just about infinite. No, what masturbation does is give you a sure way to lay down the neural pathway of orgasm.

Niels Lauerson, M.D., says in his book, *It's Your Body*, "Train yourself to recognize an orgasm when you have one. . . . The more these orgasms are trained to reflexive action, the easier it becomes to have an orgasm." Studies also show that women who masturbate have orgasms three times more easily with a partner than those who do not.

Sometimes, you may still have an uneasy feeling about masturbating. You may never have done it because of negative feelings. There is a process called the Magic Mirror that can help you acknowledge and get rid of thoughts that are stopping you. This visualization technique is effective in removing obstacles to goals you have in mind.

Using the Magic Mirror

Think of the mirror in your mind. It reflects back to you what you think. Now you see the unpleasant or old thoughts that are getting in your way. Is the feeling emotional? Body? What is the feeling exactly?

Do you feel you should save coming for your partner? Well, far from being a betrayal, knowing your own responses is an added gift, because you must know yourself to share. The first step is always to love yourself, from within.

Perhaps you feel embarrassed, or guilty.

Take whatever it is and see yourself putting it away in an ugly old vase that you always wanted to get rid of. Picture the feelings being in it, and then you putting the vase in front of the mirror of your mind. Step away, and now smash that ugly thing to smithereens! Good!

Now visualize the mirror covered with a coating of glass cleaner. Take up a sponge and mentally wipe the mirror clean, section by section. Concentrating on this is very difficult and requires great focus. It is a successful process, for example, in the treatment of migraines. Use it here to get rid of ideas bothering you.

Now visualize you in that clean, shiny mirror. Now it has a white satin frame. In it with you, visualize your solution, that is, sex without guilt. See it clearly, and now move away confidently.

Studies of people who achieve goals show that they had previously visualized their success. Seeing your success is a key method to achieving it.

Your Orgasm

Think of the masturbation process as pure pleasure. Self-pleasuring gives you respect for and delight in your body. It's not a rehearsal for orgasm, it's the real thing.

For this process, you'll need about forty-five minutes: half hour spent pleasuring yourself, the rest to enter and exit your comfort zone, the sensual room of your own. Check your daily schedule and plan ahead. Many women choose mid-morning (if their kids are in school), others like late afternoon, after class, or late in the evening, after work is over for the day. There should be no distractions, no phones to answer, no knocks on the door, no errands to run. Privacy is essential.

Begin by entering your sensuous room, and sustain that sensual environment you created. See in it your mind as well. You are building the connection between sensation, your senses, and orgasm. And now, since you've made the commitment to come, know that you will, and then place the expectation of the orgasm deep inside your heart. It's a given.

Undress, sip some wine, listen to music, smell your flowers, and relax comfortably on your bed. Begin the breathing exercises at the same time as you tense and relax every part of your body. Focus on draining tension and worries from your body and your mind. Let yourself sink into the bed as you drift off into the kingdom of your senses. Picture yourself being completely sexually satisfied. Think of every thought you had this past week that created sexual arousal, and now focus on your three special excitement triggers. Go over each one and choose your favorite. Once you've selected it, concentrate on doing the love muscle exercise that you bonded with it. Stay focused on the special sexy thought and clench your love muscle to the rhythm of the exercise you choose. Let the thought and the erotic stirrings of your pelvis meld together, each one imprinting on the other. Keeping your eyes closed now, take your hands and gently run them all over your body. Do the fingertip touching process, only this time fondle your breasts. Caress your nipples; place a finger in your mouth to soak up the moisture and then trace light soft circles around your nipples, brushing your fingers in a gentle breathing motion against them until they become erect. Then take your protruding nipple and gently or firmly rub it between your thumb and forefinger. Keep your hot thought consciously in your mind . . . think of all the times this past week that you felt sexual excitement from it. Now keep on clenching your muscle in the comfortable pace you discovered this week; feel your breathing rate increase; feel the blood pouring into your pelvis as your muscles start to tense. Take your time, you have plenty.

Now cease consciously doing your love muscle exercises and instead take your hands and move them over your breasts, down to your bellybutton over your belly. Let those wonderful hands—the doers in life—caress every inch of your pelvis . . . and now have them feel your pelvic hair as they gently separate the lips of your vagina while they begin to stroke your inner lips and your clitoris. You may move your fingers deep inside your vagina, to increase your pleasure, and perhaps stroke and stimulate your Gräfenberg spot. Now choose your second favorite turn-on and begin to do the exercises that you practiced with pleasure this past week . . . keep caressing your vulva. Use a variety of pressures and rhythms as you allow yourself to rise higher and higher in sexual excitement. Clench your muscle to the beat you learned this week . . . gradually the tension increases in your thighs and pelvis . . . you feel as if you are literally breathing with your vagina. Let yourself be open to receiving as much pleasure as you want. When you think you've had enough, don't stop. Instead, push yourself to try just one more contraction . . . deeper, higher. Meanwhile, keep caressing your inner/outer lips and of course the pure pleasure center of your vagina . . . your clitoris. Take it and gently massage it as you like best between your thumb and forefinger, just as you massaged your nipple. Relax for a moment . . . stop the exercise and feel your clitoris become engorged with the vitalizing blood . . . feel it grow between your fingers, and now as you tease it by sensual playful strokes, focus on the third hot thought and begin your exercise that you connected to it this past week. Keep stroking your vulva as you think and feel sexual excitement, feel the tension build and fill your entire body at the same time your love muscle expands with sexual excitement, muscle tension, and engorged blood vessels. It fills your pelvis . . . and then feel your erect clitoris . . . feel all of the sensations at the same time and ride the crest of the wave . . . allow yourself to skim over the top and then let go, release the energy, release the desire, release the tension, release the thought. As you do, know that you trust yourself completely and love yourself as well. Now, once you let go, feel the contractions of your love muscle (.8 per second) moving to its natural involuntary rhythm, observe the warm surge of blood flooding your pelvis and the sensations of floating calm and serene. You are one at this moment. Memorize the feeling and know that you made it happen, that you will do it again and again as you express your love for your body and your mind.

In the afterglow of creating your orgasm, lie peacefully and savor the sensations. Rest in your sensual room, resting before coming back. Feel good about yourself, rest your hand on your vulva and relax.

If you have not yet reached orgasm, that's okay. A large part of this chapter is in its atmosphere of sexuality. For almost everyone, this is the first time they have consciously tried to think about their orgasm. It's new to think technically about it as we have been doing. But it is very freeing. Take your time.

You may enjoy any of a myriad of other masturbatory situations. Use water or the shower spray, or hug a pillow between your legs. Feel easy about changing the elements, finding new combinations to give you pleasure.

Afterglow

Surely you feel a change in yourself, something gentle. Slowly, as you consider it, you begin to assume control over your involuntary responses. There is so much pleasure ahead for you in your relationship with a partner, once you feel your own creative power. Yet stay a minute longer whole and entire with your sexuality, and own it.

In *A Week on the Merrimac River*, Thoreau said, "We need pray for no higher heaven than the pure senses can furnish, a purely sensuous life. Our present senses are but rudiments of what they are destined to become." He was speaking of all our senses, but the same is true of our sexuality. Now you can coast on to the section on partnering, including exercises for the advanced, fun and games fantasy.

CHAPTER 5

Intimacy:
The Excitement of
Sharing with a Partner

The excitement of sharing with a partner can be both verbal and nonverbal. Together you can create ecstasy. Ecstasy is the essence of this chapter, even though it's something no one can define. Ecstasy is action—you'll never know it until you experience it.

This chapter is your guide to sexual pleasure, from intimate communication, the verbal skills of loving, to sexual delights. You are your partner's guide; sharing love muscle control with your partner is your pleasure.

Partnering: Life in the Fast Lane

A lot of us feel like the Red Queen, running as fast as possible just to stay in place. Sometimes we make love fast, fast, fast.

In today's culture people take contact when they can get it, hit and run. The biggest problem for our sexuality in this setting is that we want physical closeness to be immediate. It's the simplest way *not* to be close, yet still make contact with another human being. Touch is healing, yet we often have no families, no structures, to support us in a way of seeking it. Intimacy, in the old sense of the word, is hard to find. Most of us don't have a code of sexual ethics to live by.

An Intimacy Code

What is your sexual morality? Are you honest? As you prepare to share with a partner, here is a code of sexual morality that will help you toward intimacy.

● Be honest with yourself first and then risk being honest with your partner. Be naturally yourself.

● Don't do anything that makes you uncomfortable. If you feel uncomfortable, let your partner know. Own your discomfort and don't blame it on your partner. Also make it clear that you aren't rejecting him.

● You give yourself orgasm; it is not the responsibility of your partner.

● Ask your partner to let you know what feels good to him.

● When your partner is touching you you may notice any of the following signs of anxiety: dry mouth; increased heart beat; wet palms; shallow breathing;

nausea. These are signals that there is an emotional charge about the part of the body being touched. It may have sustained physical or emotional trauma in the past. If you notice this happening, concentrate on what memory arises. Be aware of any strong emotions tied to specific parts of your body.

Freedom of Sexual Choice: With a Partner of Your Choice

You have the option to share what you want with a partner. I don't want to encourage you to extend yourself beyond your own limits. One person might feel comfortable sharing all the following exercises with a new lover, another would only want to be with someone known and trusted. It's safe and smart to be aware of your present level of sexual and sensual risk-taking. None of us feel the same sexually every day. You can set limits and communicate them to your partner, according to whether you feel like experimenting or not.

Enhancing Your Relationship With Your Partner

When it comes to making a relationship last, the real experts are people who have lived a long time together in a relationship they find satisfying.

From such couples, researchers have learned that the chief difference between long-lasting satisfactory relationships and unsatisfactory relationships is the difference in the quality and openness of their communication.

Following is a chart of the specific attitude differences between these couples.

Factors that Make a Relationship Last

Long-term, satisfactory relationships showed these characteristics:	Unsatisfactory relationships showed many of these characteristics:
1. A caring love relationship	1. Fear of failure
2. Affection	2. Use of sex in a power struggle
3. Responsibility for their own sexual satisfaction	3. Poor body image
4. Knowledge of physiology of sex	4. Ambivalent feeling toward division of sex roles in the relationship
5. Confidence in their own sexual identity and sex roles	5. Rigid, stereotyped, *differing* sex value systems
6. Openness to experimentation and flexibility in sex value system	6. Poor perception of partner's image of themselves
7. Open and trusting partners as far as whatever their value system	7. Judgmental in attitude toward self
8. Nonjudgmental when confronted with sex lifestyles different from their own	8. Manipulative in sexual relationships
	9. Controlling in sexual relationships

Long-term, satisfactory relationships showed these characteristics:	Unsatisfactory relationships showed many of these characteristics:
9. Comfortable with body image	10. Utilize their partner as a sex thing or toy
10. Comfortable with their own sexual life cycle	11. Sex without love or caring
11. Comfortable with partner's perception of his or herself as a sexual person and performer	12. Sex without self-responsibility for their own satisfaction
12. Interested in their partner's satisfaction as with one's own needs.	13. Sex without affection
	14. Overly romantic attitudes toward human sexual response
	15. Ignorance of human sexual physiological responses
	16. Fear of aging

Adapted from research and list copyrighted by Patricia Schiller, J.D., sex educator, past president of the American Society of Sex Educators, Counselors and Therapists (ASSECT).

Behind the Doors
of a Sex Clinic

You might like to know what sort of information is considered routinely important to realize about yourself and your partner at a sex clinic. It gives you an idea of what are the range of factors that affect your sex life.

There are hundreds of possible answers to these questions. But by comparing yours with the list of what makes for a satisfactory intimate relationship, you can see ways in which your attitudes and experiences affect *your* relationship.

Taking a Sex History

The questions on this short form can be used to obtain the essence of the client's sexual lifestyle and values. It is also a useful tool in determining which areas of a client's sex history need to be pursued. In other words, it is a screening device.

1. How do you feel about being a woman (man)? How do you feel about the opposite sex?
2. How do you feel about your body? How do you think/feel that your partner feels about your body?
3. What was your first pleasurable sexual experience prior to puberty? What have you discussed with your partner about their preadolescent sexual experience?
4. What type of formal or informal sex education have you had? From whom? What is your partner's experience?
5. Describe your first experience with menstruation (a woman). Describe your first experience of ejaculation (either).
6. When did you first experience orgasm? Describe the experience.

7. Describe your experience with masturbation. At what age?

8. What variations in sex play do you feel comfortable with? What variations does your partner or partners feel comfortable with? Which do you enjoy the most?

9. What are your feelings about homosexuality? How does your partner feel about homosexuality?

10. What type of birth control do you use? What type do you prefer? How does your partner feel about them? What does your partner prefer?

11. How do you feel about sexual intercourse for persons over fifty?

Sex Equity

What's legal isn't always what's fair. That's why in law there's a principle called "equity." A special court decides on matters of equity, where the dispute and the decision are based not on questions of law but on what's fair. Equity is an important concept for a relationship. For all too much of history, women have been treated inequitably, because the economic power in the household belonged to the male.

When you balance the scales in a love relationship, it should have nothing to do with money. If it does, then you're still in the position of someone wielding power. The bill payer doesn't have more rights in a sexual relationship. Equity in human terms has to do with who listens.

One of the applications of these ideas is called equity theory. Psychologist Dr. Elaine Hatfield of the University of Hawaii asks people to assess their relationships according to a scale of how equitably they feel they are treated.

Try this on your relationship:

Considered as a whole, what you put into it and what you get from it, and the same for your partner, how does your total relationship "stack up"?*

+ 3 I am getting a much better deal than my partner.
+ 2 I am getting a somewhat better deal.
+ 1 I am getting a slightly better deal.
  0 We are both getting an equally good, or bad, deal.
−1 My partner is getting a slightly better deal.
−2 My partner is getting a somewhat better deal.
−3 My partner is getting a much better deal than I am.

How to Score:
  +3 +1 = Overbenefited
    0   = Equitably treated
  −3   −1 = Underbenefited

When people feel their relationships are equitable, they are more content than people who feel either overbenefited or underbenefited. (This theory has already had applications in labor relations.) They also have more satisfying sexual relations. Hatfield reports,

*Hatfield Global Measure.

"They [feel] most loving and close after sex and as-
sumed their partner felt that way too."

The study showed that "regardless of gender, those
in equitable relationships were having sexual intercourse." Most couples in inequitable relationships
were not, both the greatly overbenefited and the
greatly underbenefited. Hatfield concluded, "If couples feel *equitably treated*, sex will go well. Men and
women who feel underbenefited may find their anger
makes it difficult for them to respond sexually to
their partners. They may respond sadistically or
passive-aggressively to sexual advances." The overbenefited, "plagued with guilt over their good fortune,"
may find it hard to receive still more pleasure from
their partners.

"It's not nice to fool Mother Nature." Fair play
works best for sex.

Such attitudes only flourish in an equitable relationship. In the communication processes that follow,
each speaker is put in a position of equity. That will
help close the gap between men and women—it is
my aim to let the sexes get back together!

Communication:
The Art of Intimacy

The key to sensual pleasure is verbal and nonverbal
communication. As you say what you want, feel your
partner's pleasure and he yours, all the nuances of
mood and response are transmitted between you.

Your mutual verbal skills are as important as the physical. Sometimes the old male/female stereotypes carry over into what we do in bed, and we feel we must act according to "normal" roles. As Alex Comfort has recognized, "What's the norm in human sexuality? There is no 'norm.' Norm is the name of a guy who lives in Brooklyn!"

It's interesting to see what "norms" affect you in sexual communication, and how your partner thinks. Here are some ways you can find out.

Opening Communication: Labeling Your Sexual Stereotypes

Sit down together, and set a timer for five minutes for each answer. Ask your partner the following questions. Each person can take up to but no longer than five minutes to answer. (Setting an automatic limit is a lot better than it sounds—it gives a person confidence. They're often quite relieved to know they'll have a full five minutes to be listened to, without interruption). The other partner makes *no comment*. (If you feel this will be difficult, you may want to write down your answers separately first.)

When each of you answers, be as spontaneous as possible—say or write the first image that pops into your head. Do not change answers. If you finish before your time is up in five minutes, then don't say anything. There is no need to fill the space. Let yourself breathe, relax. Your partner, too, needs the freedom to complete his answers in the allotted time. Stretch, smile, get yourself a glass of wine.

Do You Act Differently with Men and Women?

How Do You Share	With Same Sex	With Opposite Sex
Hellos		
Goodbyes		
Expressing anger—what if you get a ticket from a cop? from a metermaid?		
Sadness		
Happiness or joy?		
Feelings of love		
Feelings of lust		
Warmth and affection		
Physical contact—for example, a handshake		
Annoyance		
A shopping trip		
Lovemaking—how do you initiate sex?		
Money—how do you handle it?		
Amount of time spent with men versus amount of time with women		
Household chores		
Jealousy		
Competition—sports, job		
Going out to dinner		
Discussing political differences		
Power disputes—at work, at home		

What is important about your answers is that they reveal your attitudes toward sexual stereotypes. As you share your answers, sexual stereotypes and sex roles are revealed. Historically, men have been the doers and women the feelers in life; your answers probably reflect this. These differences are entrenched in history and your upbringing. They are so important that when they are transported into sex, they can ruin it. Sexy is free; you must feel relaxed enough to sink into the pleasure of your own sensations, and do whatever you want to increase this pleasure. It stops being fun if you have to check in the rulebook. Stereotypes block your ability to express your common humanness and share it with a partner.

How to Talk

There's another reason this process is valuable. When you talk about hard subjects, and your partner just listens, and vice versa, as we did in this exercise, that is called nondemand communication. It's a main skill of listening and talking, and it's surprisingly hard to do. We always think we ought to jump in and offer a solution. That we're being asked to tell the other person what to do about it. Nondemand gives him a chance to consider what *he* wants to do. What matters is that we care enough to *really* listen.

Nondemand speaking is a way to say what you think or feel without making any demand on the listener about it. You are not making a list of demands; the listener is not required to act, or even respond. All he has to do is take the time and care enough to hear you out. This experience builds trust.

The other skill of verbal communication is "owning your feelings." It means you make a conscious decision to start your sentences with the word "I" if you are going to talk about a feeling. For example, "I don't like when you do that," instead of "You always do that." That way it's you who owns the feeling, not somebody else who is to blame for "making you" feel that way. If you want to be listened to by the other person, you do have to own your own feelings as you answer their questions. The words people listen to best are "*I* think" or "*I* feel." They turn off with the speed of summer lightning if you start statements with "*You* did" or "*You* didn't."

To Talk or Not to Talk

Studies show that married women who have better sex lives are ones who are able to talk about sex with their husbands. They have more frequent and better sex. They are also more satisfied with their marriages. So I'm going to talk about sex, explicitly, and give you ways to say exactly what you want and feel.

Here is a journal update to focus on what you feel about your own sexuality. I hope you continue in the pride and pleasure of your value as a sexual being. This will remind you again of your communication with your *own* body and its reactions, and confidence in your own right to have sexual needs. Then you can exchange information with a partner.

What are some of your definitions of pleasure?_____

_____

What are some of your definitions of intimacy? (Example, sexual intercourse, long talks)_____

_____

Are you continuing with your love muscle exercise schedule?_____

Are you by now up to doing them twice a day for twenty minutes a session?_____

Have you found they increase your desire?_____

Has it become easier to orgasm?_____

Do you clench to a hot bond? (chapter 4)_____

If not, do you associate clenching with observing or visualizing a turn-on?_____

Which love muscle exercise do you find the most helpful to increase sexual arousal? In general_____
Before intercourse_____ Before masturbation_____

What was your experience with the masturbation process?_____

How do you feel after coming?_____

Did you identify your Gräfenberg spot?_____
Did stroking it feel pleasurable?_____

Do guilty feelings inhibit your full participation in creating orgasm?_____

Did you use the Magic Mirror process of creative visualization to release negative feelings?_____
To visualize new wishes?_____

How often have you repeated the masturbation exercise?_____

Your journal updates help you keep in mind *who* is this person doing the communicating. They also help you keep a record of your progress in your love muscle program. The answers you have just given help remind you of your new wants and needs, your new skills in sex. Now we can address the issue of communicating aspects of your sexuality with the partner of your choice.

Two Roadblocks to Talking About Sex

Two patterns of communication are such roadblocks to sharing that they deserve special mention. These are the "Rescue Game" and "Mindreading."

The Rescue Game

This game describes many people's sexual situation.

Carmen Kerr, in *Sex for Women*, notes Dr. Claude Steiner's idea of how the game goes. It's a kind of triangle. Whatever point you're at, you can always switch to one of the others. The three points are rescuer, victim, and persecutor.

It works this way. One of the partners has a problem. The most common ones are: her orgasm— "You don't come." "You don't come fast enough"; his penis—"You ejaculate prematurely, you don't stay hard long enough." The rescuer identifies the problem. Because he or she is stronger, or is guilty, he or she rescues. It's a big mistake. Rescuing sounds like this: "That's OK, dear, I don't mind if you didn't come,

I'll just try some more. You just try to relax." Or, "That's OK, darling, I don't mind if you come so fast. I enjoy sex anyway. Besides, my orgasms aren't as important as yours."

What you'd expect from the one who got rescued is resentment. And you'll get it. But the surprise is what comes next. The *rescuer* starts persecuting the one he or she rescued. Persecuting is very familiar. It goes like this: "I've waited six months for you to come around, and if you don't do something about your problem of not coming, it's going to break up our marriage." Or, "What's wrong with *you?* You don't make me come. I don't want any more sex with you. You're a bad lover."

What to do about it? Stop rescuing! *If you rescue, you will punish*. Instead, read on! Any of the communication processes in this chapter will provide the means to stop rescuing.

Mindreading

This problem is a plague. It involves trying to read your partner's mind, like Svengali. What does he want? Doesn't he know what you want? Because our culture doesn't teach us how to talk to each other about delicate and sensitive areas, we often wind up misreading the message our partner sends us.

What gets the ball rolling again is if both of you make a commitment to disclose your feelings *at the moment*, even if they are *negative*. The problems created by mindreading can be avoided, or negotiated, and resolved. All relationships run the gamut of emotions; you're bound not to like something! It's okay to let your partner know what you do or don't like. You pay him the compliment of trusting that he can take it. Then you can negotiate. And it's such a relief when you clear something up between you.

Talking About the Basics

When it gets right down to talking explicitly about sex, most people fall back fifteen yards and punt. They also fall back fifteen centuries. It takes a little courage to start the conversation. The following process is the one I have found makes it easiest and most valuable for partners to talk explicitly about sex.

The process helps you reveal your sexual expectations. Each question should be asked four times—each answer seems to bring out a different side of the truth. (Some of these questions make for an interesting bar game, as a way to get to know what a person is like.) Since you are doing this process together, it really makes it easy for you to talk about you and sex.

Tell Me, What Are Your Sexual Needs? Can You Risk Doing That?

Ask your partner each question four consecutive times. Listen attentively to the answer. Make the answers as succinct as possible—one or two words if you can. Hold hands, look at each other, and urge your partner to answer spontaneously.

1. What words do you use to describe sex and the parts of your body?
2. What is it like to be a man? ⎫ Ask these regardless
3. What is it like to be a woman? ⎬ of the sex of the person talking!
4. What is it like for you to be a sex partner?
5. What is your greatest sexual pleasure?
6. What is your greatest sexual fear?
7. What do you want to do in bed?
8. What do you want your lover to do in bed?
9. What time of the day do you feel sexy?
10. What way do you like best to come?
11. How do you like to masturbate?
12. What sexual needs do you have trouble communicating? Say it now.
13. What is your sexual fantasy?

Your commitment in this process is *to listen, whether or not you like what you hear*. The point is not to do anything about it, just to hear the person out and be heard. It means you care about something important to the other person. Ask your partner, "How do you feel about this?" "How do you feel about me asking you such personal questions?" Hold hands for a minute.

Now, can you give each other mutual permission to explore sex in the way you prefer? It's also okay to say no, too, isn't it?

If This Process Didn't Work

There are some things you can do that will defeat that sexiest of all things, communication. They are all variations of not listening. Review the following list, and try to catch yourself and stop them as you do the exercise over again.

When your partner shares, you might

1. Pretend to listen
2. Interrupt
3. Offer a solution to a problem
4. Stop listening if you feel threatened
5. Stop listening if you feel criticized
6. Go over the set time limit, hogging (controlling) the process
7. Stop (withdraw from) physically touching (staying in contact) with your partner
8. Criticize your partner's answers
9. Not concentrate on your partner's answers
10. Not be committed to listen
11. Be thinking of your answer while your partner is speaking (the pounce)
12. Grimace, frown, giggle, or scratch
13. Finish their sentence for them
14. Collect scores for later arguing
15. Blame your partner
16. Blame his mother
17. Refuse to own your own feelings

Be as open and honest as possible. Be straight. This is a chance to really get to know your partner better, discover how sex roles and stereotypes may have influenced your communication, and find out what you'd really like to do in sex.

And it won't make you a traffic cop in bed.

Now let's go on to the ineffable physical delights of love.

The Art of Love

Set aside time to be together, prime time, in your sensuous space, and prepare to call on and awaken all of your senses. You may feel freer with a new partner, or be eager to explore with someone familiar. Once you begin these processes, you will see facets in each other of the kind that keep people hotly sexual together for a lifetime.

Subtle Erotic Teasers

Touch Anticipation

Here is a way of sensing touch prior to its actually happening, of knowing how a touch or sensation feels so that even in your memory you lay down the neural pathway and make the mind-body connection. Pay attention, and remember what you feel.

While you are both dressed, stand face to face, and

put your hands up as if to a mirror. The other person is the image. The tease is not to touch, just move your hands as your partner moves his, bending and moving as if you were touching each part of each other's body, even kneeling down to move over legs and thighs. This is an exercise in letting the other person lead. It helps you to learn their rhythms, and vice versa.

Almost all societies use dancing as a ritual before lovemaking, as we do. Dancing serves to set up erotic rhythms and touch, display the body, and pump up blood.

Did it feel warm or tingle when your lover passed your hands over some parts of your body? Did your skin feel as if it would jump out and pull your partner's hands to you? How close could your hands get? Did you laugh? (Of course you laughed.)

Stand Pat

Let some garments slither to the floor, and take your partner's hands. Guide them to touch parts of your body. All they do is cup and touch, nothing more. They sort of pat you. The purpose here is not to come but to let you sink into your feelings and feel connected with each other.

A Nonsexist Strip

Women, as we said, frequently express the wish to be able to turn the tables and watch *men* strip. Now places where men strip have been opening up around

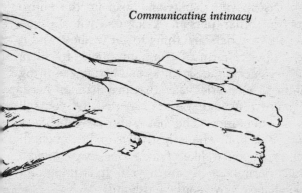

Communicating intimacy

the country. It's something you, too, may enjoy seeing and doing with your partner in your own home. So, slowly take your clothing off in front of him and vice versa, or you can undress each other. Put on some music. Tell him how you like to look at him, and let him tell you.

Erotic Shower

Usually your shower is probably a five-minute scrub. Try going into the shower for other purposes. A shower is mysterious by candlelight; it feels as though your sense of touch is heightened. Use some nice soap, something pleasing to the skin; have some soft towels hung up. Offer him (and he you) a sweet from a little dish you set down. Taste it on his mouth. This is a special experience you are going to share. In a sensual shower, you both will give and receive.

Stand under the shower in turn and then hug, full-body. Try to press your bodies together, ankle to lips. Then soap your hands and soap up the entire body of the other person. A lot of trust goes on here—it's a very personal thing to get washed, and it can be a special form of communication. In all of these experiences, the slowness and caring can bring up childhood memories, and that may happen here. As the water runs and you are caressed, let yourself feel these memories. The hot water may be very soothing. Ask him where he'd like to be touched, and tell what you'd like. Guide the soapy hands. Give him permission to touch you. It is important that your hands move softly and lightly.

Wash each other's genitals, and linger over the buttocks or breast. Try to increase your tactile response, feel what he is feeling. It is amazing how much feeling you can get through a hand when you put all your attention on what you are feeling. Concentrate on the pleasure his hand is giving you.

It is okay not to like something. You know how to own your own feelings. If something feels uncomfortable or weird, say, "I am not comfortable," or "I don't like that." You have permission from each other to share what you feel. Focus on what you like. Turn to hug his back, feel the rounds of his buttocks. Feel yourself fitting together. Come out when you want to and pat dry.

Your Body, My Body

These processes are done without goals. They are a way to heighten your sensations, and they are fulfilling in themselves. You are not rushing through them to get to something else; they take whatever time they take. Sink into them, sense the erotic nature of your whole body. You'll notice with each passage there is a quieting of the kind of worrying and thinking that amounts to a kind of "noise" in your brain.

In chapter 2 you learned to accept your body. As you dry off, stand before a mirror together, in the soft light of your sensuous room, and let the towels fall. Run your hands over the erotic body of your

partner and look in the mirror. It's not what you
have, it's the style in which you flaunt it! Pose, strut
around, look at each other in the mirror. Hug. People usually notice when doing this that they have
feelings of increasing recognition and respect for their
own body.

Try now to be as aware of the other as when you
listened, only this time watch your own and his body
movements. Are shoulders tensed up, face frowning,
movements nervous? Let yourselves see perceptively.
Notice the environment, the candles, the perfume.
It is amazing how people respond to a sensual
environment.

Hills and Valleys—The Back Caress

Lie down on your stomach. You can decide who
will go first. Feel the soft sheets, and feel the comfort of the room. Your partner straddles you and sits
on your behind or just below it on the thighs. He
sprinkles power or massage oil lightly over your back,
then lightly explores it. The purpose of this exercise
is to take the longest time possible, five or ten minutes,
to explore with your fingertips every facet of his body
from the back, skipping the genitals. Sit between his
legs and explore the thighs from knee to crotch, trace
up and down behind the knees, up the lower back.

Then reverse roles.

Watch out for his weight in this sensual delight. If
he is much heavier, he may make you feel very
overpowered. You may be unable to move. It can

take away the pleasurable aspects of this slow exploration. If you have an inordinate fear of being imprisoned (and many women exposed to rape have these feelings), he should sit to the side of you.

Follow his hands as he gets lost in his own sensations of pleasure in touching you. Let your mind follow just under the skin everywhere he goes, and feel the pleasure of the sensations.

Face Caress

Touch his face lightly, notice the texture and the warmth, taking five minutes to explore all the planes and angles as though the face were a foreign country. Be careful about closing off the nose. Lightly pinch the eyebrows between your fingers, doing both simultaneously. Softly stroke eyelids, eyelashes. We forget the details of a face.

As your face is explored, concentrate on how it feels to you. It should feel as though you are being nurtured. Considered what memories it brings to mind.

I Love to Go A-Wandering

Wander on to the back of the neck, the upper chest, not the nipples, on to the legs, the toes. You can use lotion as you journey down the body. If you have a dislike or distaste for semen, lotion (which feels similarly wet and slippery on the body yet is nonthreatening) can be used reassuringly in the hands of your lover to desensitize you to that fear.

Sexological Exam

Purpose

To demystify what the female anatomy is. This exam shows there is nothing inside to hurt the male. By this exploration you will also find out where the most erogenous areas are. More sensations will be aroused, and you will find new ways to prolong your sexual experiences by finding your and partner's areas of sensitivity. Everyone has erotic areas outside the usual.

Studies show that couples had more and more frequent sex after erotic touching than after watching erotica.

The male explores your body first. He gently spreads your legs, inquires if you are comfortable. He feels your pubic hair, its texture, then asks you to name the parts he is touching and caressing. It is a dialogue between you.

In some women the inner lips are as sensitive as the clitoris. Tell him how you like to be touched.

Feedback

The man wets his finger by sucking it and gently traces the rims of your areolas. Are they light? Dark? How do they feel? Do your nipples become erect? Your breasts? Does one breast feel any different than the other? Does the sensitivity of your breasts change during the month? Most women report extreme variation in pleasurable sensations from breast caresses during their monthly cycle. Is your partner aware of these fluctuations of sensation? Tell your partner how you feel, and that your breasts feel different during the month.

Self-blame, partner misunderstanding (What have I done wrong this time? or, She liked this last week, why not tonight?), can be simply resolved with information and a sensible sensual exam of your erogenous zones.

Use your body as a biofeedback machine. Listen to your body. Acknowledging and understanding its messages and transmitting your feelings to your partner are the basis of integrated intimacy.

Your partner moves again to touch your vagina. First he touches the top, and asks you to help him find the clitoris. It can be hard to find. Men often think, Well, I'll just rub around, it's in the area, but they may miss or hit the top, which hurts. Tell him what you like. Pull back at the conjunction of the lips, and press that back toward your belly; it should begin to swell and pop up. If not, keep going down, pulling the lips back, to where the lips join, until you see the clitoris. It should move freely if there are no adhesions. You can show him the urethra, a tiny pinhole below the clitoris, the vagina, the perinium, all sensitive.

He inserts a finger in your vagina. Taking the top as 12 o'clock he moves his finger as if around a clock to determine what areas of the love muscle are most sensitive. As he does, you give him feedback. Scientists used to believe that the 4 and 8 o'clock positions (at the lower part) of the vagina were the most exciting to women, but the evidence now is that the upper part is much more sensitive to thrusting, around the 1 or 2 o'clock position (the upper part under the bone). Women report they like the pressure up at the top, which is consistent with the location of the Gräfenberg spot. He places his finger one or two finger joints in and you squeeze. Notice that the depth of penetration doesn't matter. This is used in sensual awareness training (sex therapy) to reassure a man with a small penis. He can still give pleasure by stimulating your love muscle. You can receive stimulation by contracting around even a small penis.

Your Gräfenberg Spot

No researcher who knows how to look has yet found a woman without one! The Gräfenberg spot may come in any size, from flat and the size of a dime to puffed up and larger than a half-dollar, but every woman so far examined for it has one.

One woman reported hers was so large that it was a source of embarrassment to her. She would reach orgasm when her doctor examined her internally, since touching it was unavoidable. Some women's Gräfenberg spots have even been surgically removed as an unexplained swelling on the urethra.

Some women have volunteered that they believe stimulation of their Gräfenberg spot to be their only known way of coming. But most women have no idea that their Gräfenberg spot is there. You may be an ejaculator, in which case you already know it, depending on how powerfully the ejaculate is expelled. You may or may not connect ejaculating with stimulation of the spot. Most ejaculators do. Some researchers would also call an ejaculation any sudden release of the fluid, which you may have experienced, or experience regularly. Have you experienced anything like that since starting love muscle exercises? They powerfully increase stimulation to the Gräfenberg spot.

I believe many women to be "retrograde ejaculators," meaning they hold the fluid in when they come and probably eject it back into the urethra and bladder because of their fear of wetting the bed. Ask your lover to stimulate the spot.

The Gräfenberg spot can be covered up by the rim of a vaginal diaphragm. You can only try to palpate it when you have nothing in you. Your lover places his fingers up inside the vagina as you lie either propped up or with your legs up. Feel the ribbed love muscle, then a smooth spot on the upper surface of the vagina, halfway between the rim of the pubic bone and the cervix. It actually can be located anywhere along that line, although most seem to be a little closer to the opening of the vagina. He presses *very firmly* upward, trying to locate an area that is not ribbed. It is round in shape and feels not muscular but glandular. He strokes this spot by pressing it very hard, until it starts to swell. At first it will feel intensely uncomfortable, creating a burning feeling as if you're going to urinate any minute. That will not happen. Ask him to report what is happening. You may notice a continuing stream of clear juice appearing, running down between the buttocks. This is considered intensely erotic by some partners. Many women say that they quickly feel an almost overpowering urge to orgasm, and indeed that it is inevitable if the stimulation is continued. Women also report (and Perry and Whipple cite in their research) that they orgasm from stimulation in the top third of their vagina, the area including the Gräfenberg spot and the cervix (opening of the uterus). For those women who have orgasms from the upper third of the vagina, stimulation of the inside of the vagina, with a penis or a sexual device (chapter 7) is *critical*. So the width and length of the penis *does* matter to some women, in light of this evidence. As the Gräfenberg spot grows in size, and you come close to orgasm, you may feel a strong urge to perform what is called the Valsalva Maneuver. This is a sudden downpush like the downpush in the push and pull love muscle exercise, such that the urinary opening is turned outward. Women who reach an orgasm in this way suddenly push down and forceably eject a quantity of clear fluid, ejaculating the exact duplicate of male ejaculate without sperm. Try pushing down hard, as your partner stimulates you. If this produces an ejaculation, that is quite normal. If the stimulation is pleasant, although you do not feel like coming, feel the sensation from inside and try to consider what you feel as tiny orgasms. Orgasm from Gräfenberg spot stimulation has been reported by some women as feeling quite different from that in other areas, and some consider it specifically uterine. After this exploration, rest.

Funny Places

It is normal to be quite turned on at this point of the sexological exam. That's a main point of it. Yet a lot of women have a sort of mini-dead zone almost equal in unresponsiveness to the area from the hips to the thighs. These areas of the body feel as if they just had a shot of anesthetic, or else they're ticklish. You tend to keep someone away from them. *Those* are the very areas that are likely to be the most erotic on your body. They can be awakened.

The most common are the:

belly		back of the neck
buttocks	often ticklish	ears
armpits		back of the knees
back		

If you relax and let go consciously, all these areas are sensual. If you notice that you do respond, learn to let go and trust. As you do these exercises, if you notice a tendency to giggle, think of diving into a delicious cool pool of water, because it's so hot and you want to dive in and let go. Then you do it, and float on top of the water. This kind of creative visualization can help you let go and float in pleasure.

Do you know the pleasure of keeping a secret? Imagine you have a surprise for someone, something great, you save it, and then you have the pleasure of giving it to them, or the moment of telling the secret. Think of that feeling.

Secrets of a Man

Your partner lies down and spreads his legs. You look at his penis, and take it into your hand, asking him if he is comfortable. How does he like to have it held? How firmly? Look at the hole at the end. Is he circumcised or not? If he is uncircumcised, move the skin up the shaft near the round head, the glans. See his reaction. Under the crown is the corona ridge; the line running down the back of the shaft is the Raphe-midline. Touch these with fingers or tongue; also the balls (testes) in the scrotum. Ask how he likes them held or touched. They pull up during orgasm. Underneath the crown is a delicate membrane that extends about half an inch along the vein. If you lick it you will drive him wild. Then you can explore the perineum and the anus. All of these are pleasure zones. None of them are taboo.

Sometimes just knowing all the techniques isn't enough. What's been built between you here, caring, connecting your whole self, integrating your mind and body with someone else's, that's the pleasure of sex. A worthwhile intimacy is built on the willingness to take things sowly. Enjoy each other gradually, key in to being aroused with this person. Then your

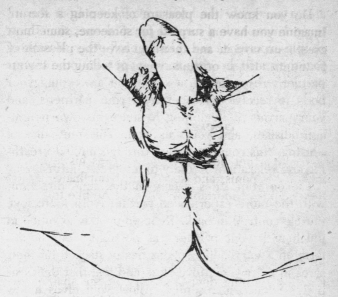

The male genitalia

sexuality unfolds slowly, where neither overwhelms or frightens the other, but the physical keeps pace with the emotional. Then there is always one more delight to uncork.

Time Out: Spoonbreathing

To use your love muscle successfully with a partner you must first and foremost relax together. Synchronized breathing (also called spoonbreathing) is an effective technique for tension reduction. It creates a peaceful, nonthreatening recess from the intense emotions and excited physical sensations most people experience in exploring each other. Breathing together also heightens your perception of your partner's response. In a sense you are tuning your body to receive messages from your partner's, and your partner is beginning to sense his own neural-aphrodisiacs, and yours as well. This mutuality of sensing, this communication through unified breathing and relaxation, is a key to integrated intimacy.

Lie on your sides, facing in the same direction, with the more experienced partner (with more love muscle control) in back. Keep your body as much in touch with your partner's as possible. Your bodies form an S curve, like spoons neatly stacked on their sides in a drawer. Move close and feel that delicious body. Silence is essential. Allow yourselves a few minutes to breathe at your own rhythm. Inhale, let the diaphragm rise, exhale, let it fall. Let the signs of stress, anxiety, and tension slip away, just like the stale attitudes and environments from which many of us have struggled to release ourselves. Let the sweet scent of you together transport you back to the serene beauty you felt when you created your own retreat. That's where you are now. Hold on to that sensation of ease and comfort.

Once totally relaxed the person in back synchronizes breathing to the breathing of the partner in front. It's helpful to have the partner in back gently place a hand on the diaphragm of his or her partner. This lets each feel the rise and fall of the abdomen in union with their own. The abdomen should push out when inhaling (expand the chest cavity to take in air) and contract (fall slightly) when you are exhaling. Breathe in unison for five minutes. Let any disturbing or distracting thoughts float through your mind, and realize that those thoughts aren't you. Try to empty your mind of all thoughts, value judgments, and other distractions. Concentrate on your breathing. Still maintain silence. After five minutes or so, change places. Again concentrate on unifying your breath for at least five minutes.

One or both of you may fall asleep. It is one of nature's oldest ways of creating security. But I hope the fun has just begun. Here the technique is used to de-stress a partner who might feel pressured learning about love muscle control.

Let's talk love muscle control in the nude. Both you and your partner are probably floating in the zone of comfortable eroticism. Maintain this peaceful state and sit up facing each other. Make eye contact, and ask how you felt about spoonbreathing. Making your love muscle work for you and with a partner is similar to synchronized breathing.

Love Muscle in Action

When your lover checked what positions felt best to you by moving his finger around the love muscle, you clenched around his finger with that loveliest of muscles, right? Now it will help to show him just how that muscle works in you before he uses his.

Take up a good (high-intensity) light and an easily held mirror, to aid in the game of getting to know your genitals. Whatever position you used, sitting in a chair with legs splayed, resting on pillows, propped up with your feet on the floor and knees up, or lying flat on your back with knees raised comfortably to your chest and slightly spread, will expose the vulva to the delighted erotic scrutiny of your partner. Assume one of these postures, and clench your love muscle as your partner watches. Think of one of those hot bonds, and clench away. Do each of the three love muscle exercises you practice alone. As you both watch the clenching motion, there will be a distinct visual difference between the slow and sustained grip, the pulse, and the push and pull. Can your *friend* tell? Ask him to describe it (visually pulling up toward the inside of your body). What about you? Have you ever watched yourself clench before? Was it helpful? When you want to clench in a certain way now, can you add the creative visualization of how it looked to the sensation you feel? Let your partner visualize the gripping around him.

A Man's Love Muscle Exercises: It's Not For Women Only

Ask the following questions to help your partner identify his love muscle.

Yes   No

1. Has he ever given a midstream urine sample? ____ ____

2. Has he ever been surprised while urinating and stopped his urine flow before his bladder was empty? ____ ____

3. Has he ever made his penis move up and down when erect (like lifting a weight or raising a drawbridge)? ____ ____

4. Is he able to have an orgasm in small batches, hold back his major ejaculation until the end during intercourse? In other words, can he separate orgasm from ejaculation? ____ ____

For many men all they need to begin ejaculatory control is to hear that it is possible. Most men have never considered it possible to separate their feelings of orgasm from ejaculating. They are glad to hear it *is* possible with love muscle control. If a man gains control of his muscle, he can increase the staying power of his erection as much as he wants (barring any physical problems). As he exercises he will find it possible to experience his orgasm gradually, a little at a time, without ejaculating. When he does, the pleasure is even more intense.

Let's hope he has anwwered yes to some of the above questions. If he hasn't, he can still learn very quickly to flex his muscle.

It's been my experience that every man who was

lucky enough to discover how to do this, or was taught, has blessed the name of the woman involved. Imagine the pleasure of gaining control over what seemed an involuntary reaction. The more a man practices, the more control he will have over his orgasm and how long he can stay hard.

Pour him a glass of water or wine, and ask him to tell you when he feels the urge to urinate. Go to the bathroom with him, and place your hand on his penis, touching the underside. Then ask him to start urinating. Once he's urinating, ask him if he would like to try and stop the flow as quickly as he can. As soon as he does, tell him, "Remember that sensation; that's the love muscle clenching." Now he can try it again and again, until the muscle memory is firmly ingrained in his brain. You can hug him while he does it, or be an encouraging spectator. He can do this part of the exercise every time he goes to the bathroom, and soon transform the feeling to the bedroom. He, like you, contracts his love muscle consciously and unconsciously many times during the day and night, and in response to whatever turns him on. Most men are absolutely fascinated when they learn how to do this, and will begin practicing as soon as they've got the information. (The only possible drawback can be too much enthusiasm too soon, leading to a sore muscle for a day or so—but the soreness goes away rapidly. So for the first week, it would be best if he exercised just ten minutes twice a day.)

To the Man

Love muscle exercises need not be elaborate. They can be very simple and very effective. The three main exercises are described below. If you feel no soreness, or very little, increase the time, working up to twenty minutes twice a day after the third week, and unlimited after that.

1. The Bathroom Exercise

Make it a habit to clench twice, completely stopping the flow each time you urinate. Be certain that you do this at least three times daily. (This is in addition to your other exercises.)

2. Clench and Hold

Clench your muscle and hold the clench for ten seconds, then clench again, hold, and release.

This exercise can be done during masturbation and before and during intercourse.

3. The Fishing Pole

Clench your muscle as hard as possible and release. Alternate clench and release as fast as possible. If you do this exercise with an erection, you will notice the penis bobs up and down like a fishing pole. A good time to do it is in the morning, before your first urination, when most men have an erection.

Do the exercises for 10 minutes twice a day, alternating exercises 2 and 3, five minutes each. Within six weeks you should reach a satisfactory level of control and achieve intensified orgasms.

Performance Anxiety (Female Division): Storm over Female Sexuality

When I told the highly respected sex researchers Hartman and Fithian, who invented the sexological exam, that I was going to explain about the love muscle and the latest information in female sexuality, such as ejaculation, they begged me to be careful. "Please don't let this become an issue of competition among women. It'll start the whole problem of performance anxiety all over again." We have seen the corrosive effects of competition over penis size and performance among men. Competition would lead to performance anxiety just as surely in women. The reason this is possible has to do with the nature of the Gräfenberg spot and the love muscle.

The evidence grows that the stronger your love muscle is the more likely it is you will ejaculate when you are either stimulated or reach orgasm. There are tribes in Africa where women shoot their ejaculate across the hut and hit the opposite wall. To put it another way, once you know about the love muscle and work on strengthening your muscles, you may discover that you ejaculate. Or you may already release floods of fluid, and just not know it. (It should be something you can ask your lover.)

But what if you do not release such fluid—and don't care if you do or not?

Some of the most recent advances in sexuality have been to apply measuring devices to gauge the strength of the vaginal muscles. Researcher Dr. John Perry links these to biofeedback machines to help a woman train her muscle. I have shown you how to apply the principles of auto-biofeedback, in which we are our own biofeedback mechanisms, without the use of a machine. But once measuring and scales by which we can make comparisons enter into the picture, the chances increase that the truth that we are all human and all sexual, in whatever way we are, will once more be overlooked.

It's already started. Some women in the field have found themselves being asked by a partner, "Won't you just ejaculate for me?" We don't *need* this kind of pressure. The last thing we need now is another model that we have to follow to perform when we're with men. It's just another stereotype! In this book we have just rid ourselves of feeling that we had to have multitudes of orgasms, or types of orgasms we couldn't have. When Masters and Johnson did their research their results helped many, but we recognize today that their evidence was already biased—the women they chose were specifically chosen *because* they had clitoral orgasms.

Those measurements are already archaic. Now we have more sophisticated hardware, microcircuitry and biofeedback machines. What we use now is like a Concorde compared to a two-engine plane.

It's soon going to be possible to obtain printed read-outs of your love muscle control, or at the least use a home biofeedback device to check its tone (see chapter 6). It is startling to see your ability to use your love muscle traced in black and white by a needle moving over a strip of graph paper. It is as obvious as a man's erection.

What's it like to be hooked up to biofeedback machines connected to your love muscle? It can create acute anxiety. As a sex therapist, I acknowledge the rediscovery of the Gräfenberg spot, but I have already personally felt pressure to perform. These measurements and machines cannot tell you whether you are a good lover, or whether you are enjoying yourself. Therefore, put this information into perspective. It is simply another indication of the infinite variety of female pleasure and orgasm.

Steps to Sharing Orgasm with a Partner

As you start the intercourse exercises, keep this code of intimacy close to your heart and be true to the messages your body and mind send you.

1. Start and end each sexual exploration session with spoonbreathing, remaining silent and concentrating on breathing in unison.

2. Observe your partner's body language.
3. Listen with total openness and attention to each other. Look into your partner's eyes when he speaks, and gently touch (maintain physical contact) your partner as he speaks.
4. Speak softly. Keep eye contact as you speak. Remember that the eyes are the receptors of the intellect and you want to communicate your thoughts and feelings to a partner who gets your message.
5. Reiterate the code of intimacy we discussed at the beginning of the chapter. Take the risk and be honest with your partner. Don't act in any way that makes your uncomfortable. Let your partner know, and own your own discomfort. Differentiate between your emotional feelings and body sensations.
6. Be aware of the sensual feelings in your body as it responds to your partner touching you. Concentrate specifically on the quality of sensation and sensitivity of each different section of your body.
7. You give yourself orgasm; it is not the responsibility of your partner.
8. Ask your partner what feels good when you touch him.

Partner Pleasure

Create a sensual mood, envelop yourself and your surroundings in the symbols of pleasure. Engage all the senses. Let go of the desire for an orgasm, and begin the process of sharing ecstasy with a partner.

Think sensually. Smell the flowers in your room, caress your breasts slowly with a love oil, touch sensual objects in your environment. Absorb every sensation. Swivel your hips to your favorite record, and memorize the feeling of touching, tasting, looking at erotic things.

After the erotic processes, touching, showering, any and all, begin these exercises with your lover.

The intent of the basic exercises for orgasm control is to create a sensory memory inside the walls of your vagina as you use your sex muscles to clench and grasp your partner's penis. Your partner will become aware of the physical sensations his penis feels as he presses it against the walls of your vagina.

The goal is to increase genital sensation. *Orgasm* is tossed out of the bedroom and your mind. All of these orgasm exercises focus your attention on the sensation of the moment. They ask you, as mentioned in the practice of touch anticipation, to memorize the sensation. To do that you must pay attention, and that keeps you in the now. Later you will use these sense anticipation memories even before intercourse as they intensify the pleasure of intercourse and orgasm.

The Slow and Sustained Grip

The position a couple chooses varies on how erect your partner's penis is. Penetration is always possible whether a penis is limp or hard as a rock. Let's start with a soft penis. Please, don't get hung up on any judgments, performance anxieties, or guilt. It's normal and quite okay to have a soft penis. Relax and enjoy what's to come.

I bet most of you didn't know that you can have sexual penetration with a limp phallus, did you? Here's your chance to learn.

STUFFING

Man lies on his side, you lie perpendicular to his penis with both legs over his hips. Your vagina touches his penis. Gradually and gently caress his penis, holding it firmly at the base. With your outer and inner lips open and moist (lubricate if necessary), insert (stuff) his penis inside your vagina. Once inside lie quietly. Your vulva at this point is pressed firmly against his pubic hair and base of his penis, your hand is no longer necessary to keep his penis inside. Now breathe in unison, before you begin the exercise.

An alternate position: man lies on his back, you sit astride and gradually (as above) insert the limp penis inside the vagina with your hand. This method is also good for men and women who are virgins. For a man it minimizes the fear that he *has* to have an erection, he can feel warm and safe and doesn't have to perform; these are important things. It also minimizes your fear of penetration. This also helps focus on how your pelvis feels, which is the point.

1. Once the penis is inside, relax by synchronizing your breathing. When you both feel comfortable, ask

your partner to clench his love muscle, hold it for three seconds, and then relax. Ask him to remember the sensation when he stopped his flow of urine, or when he flicked his penis up and down. That's the feeling you want him to repeat now. It's the slow and sustained grip exercise you learned. Now, it's his turn. As he clenches his muscle, holds it for three seconds and then relaxes, make no motion with your vagina or pelvis; keep perfectly still, and passive. Repeat this ten times, relaxing completely between contractions, by maintaining deep breathing, preferably in unison.

2. Close your eyes (this helps concentration). Gently instruct your partner to contract in the above pattern, hold three seconds, and relax. Focus on the physical sensation inside your vagina as your partner clenches and relaxes his love muscle.

TOWER OF GOLDEN RINGS: A

Visualize your vaginal barrel as a series of thin golden rings that rest upon each other. The first ring begins at the entrance to your vagina, and the last ring rests against your cervix. The rings of pure gold are slightly flexible, so when you clench against them, and the penis that snugly fits inside, they become smaller. When you relax they return to their original size. These magical golden rings are sensitive to any pressure pushing against them, as well. When your partner clenches his love muscle your sensitive golden rings notice a change of pressure and sensation inside the rings that surround his penis. Some rings are more sensitive than others, so as he clenches, try to distinguish which section of rings feels what sensation.

Can you feel his contraction in the upper third of your Golden Ring channel (vaginal barrel)?
Yes_____   No_____

Can you sense his clench in the middle of the stack of rings?
Yes_____   No_____

Can you feel his flex in the lower third of your vaginal barrel encircled with golden rings?
Yes_____   No_____

Do you notice any difference in sensation when he clenches?
Yes_____   No_____

In what area of your vagina do you feel the most sensation?
Lower_____   Middle_____   Upper_____

Is the sensation the same, when his penis contracts, throughout the circumference (inner) of the rings?
Yes_____   No_____

Does the sensation of the inner circumference that hugs his penis vary when he tightens his penis? Do you feel more in the ring that presses toward your abdomen? Do you feel more from the area of the ring that presses against your spine? Does the right side of the ring feel the same as the left side of the ring?

I certainly do not expect you to isolate all of the

preceding sensations quickly. It is very helpful, however, to know that it is possible to have sensations of varying intensity throughout your tower of golden rings, and each woman will feel different. What's important is that you can learn to isolate sensation up and down the walls and also find out what parts of your vagina feel best when a penis presses against them without thrusting. Paying attention to the sensation with a "silent" vagina helps develop a sensory memory, which you will later use before intercourse and in the advanced exercises.

Feedback

After your partner clenches his penis ask him to observe his sensations, and share them with you as the two of you relax. If he becomes erect during the slow and sustained grip, great, but still do not thrust and go for the big O. The key here is SLOW, SLOW, SLOW. He is to focus on his sensations the same as you. He should notice when his penis became erect. What areas of his penis felt more sensation? How did he feel before and after the series of ten exercises? He is also to visualize his penis growing bigger and bigger, bursting the golden tower of rings, pushing beyond the vaginal walls and up into the universe.

These questions will keep you in the now of your sensations. They reinforce the experience to put the physical exercise in a contextual framework. You remember what you feel. The vagina can feel very, very much. Memorizing the sensations helps you to focus on them.

1. Now it's your turn to contract. As your partner remains passive, start the slow and sustained grip love muscle exercise. Clench your wonderful muscle or tower of golden rings around the penis you surround with your pelvic musculature (sex muscles). You now have the power. The essence of creation is inside you. Hug your partner's penis with a firm, strong clench. Embrace his penis bottom to top and top to bottom, limp or hard. Never forget the pleasure in the process. It feels good, even without commitment. Of course, exaltation and ecstasy are only reached with the time and caring of commitment. Let thoughts of future time, sexual stereotypes, and fear dissipate as you grasp his penis internally at least ten times.

Observe your reactions and sensations, both emotional and physical. Treasure your power of control. Then relax and let yourself unclench, withdrawing his penis from your vagina. Lie quietly, keeping the sense memory of the vaginal sensation of pressing against a living, life-giving organ, his penis. Remember the joy of physical union without orgasm. Spoon breathe, rest, and relax with the excitement of future pleasure tucked silently inside your mind-body connection. You don't have to think about it, simply let it be.

When Your Partner Has an Erection

When your partner has an erect penis there are, once again, a variety of positions to select from for penetration.

1. You can lie on your back with your legs raised from the hips and rest them comfortably on his shoulders. Or you can raise your legs, bending them from your knees and rest them against your chest. Both of these positions ease penetration by opening the lips of the vagina, and the vagina itself.

2. Then there's spreading your legs as far apart as possible (it's more fun if your partner grabs your ankles and eases them apart), then as he inserts his stiff penis inside the gold rings, wrap your legs around his back, and place your arms around his neck. Once his penis is inside, both of you are to practice spoonbreathing, and lie passively. There is no motion from either partner. Be silent. Imagine yourself floating in a beautiful pond effortlessly, or think of the joy of being weightless. There is no push or pull. Orgasm is not the aim. Silent, peaceful relaxation is.

When you are both relaxed, follow the same instructions as for (the slow and sustained grip) when the partner is without erection. Ask him to clench his love muscle, hold it for three seconds, and then relax. Repeat ten times. Notice the various sensations as you passively receive his tension. Focus totally on the variation of senses inside your vagina as his penis relaxes and as it tightens. Developing a sensory memory is the goal.

3. Now it's your turn again. Ask your partner to be totally passive. Next do your slow and sustained grip love muscle exercises with whatever hold you have achieved at this point. Relax and repeat ten times. Memorize the sensations inside your vagina as you clench his erect penis with your sex muscles.

Focus only on the physical sensation; if you are at an advanced level you can try to clench (isolate) the upper third of your vagina, then the middle, and then the lower third. It's like a rippling motion, from top to bottom. Then reverse the process and clench his hard penis from the base to the head, each time using a separate set of golden rings. Remind your partner to remain totally passive (inert) during your clenching and holding exercises. When you relax, exchange feedback about the physical sensations.

Let him know it's his responsibility to tell you if he feels that ejaculation is imminent. Then use the following technique.

Squeeze Technique

If your partner tells you he is about to come, have him withdraw his penis. Immediately place your thumb on his frenulum (the area just under the head of the penis) and press for about ten seconds, he can tell you how hard. This is the famous squeeze technique of Masters and Johnson. This should stop his ejaculation and his erection. The good news is that he only loses it to gain it back again. Think of the marvelous side effect—confidence is firmly established, once he sees an erection disappear (before his very eyes, so to speak) and then experiences its reappearance. This usually happens within a few moments.

When he is limp, use the first slow and sustained grip technique, then continue the love muscle exercise. You go first, while he remains passive. Then switch.

Most likely after you squeeze his penis three to four times his erection will return harder than ever.

After each of you has gone through at least ten repeats of clench and hold slow and sustained grip while your partner remains passive, stop the exercise, and assume the curved, cuddling spoonbreathing position. Rest, relax, and hold on to the sensory memory created by touching each other deep inside your body.

TOGETHER

Follow the most comfortable position you used in either of the preceding exercises. Next, after unifying your breathing patterns, contract your love muscles together, hold for at least three seconds, relax, and hold each other. Kiss and breathe. Repeat simultaneous contractions ten times. Focus only on the feelings, the physical sensations; visualize the golden rings pressing tightly. Now press with the uppermost of the rings, kiss, and relax.

Eighty-five percent of American women, according to Hartman and Fithian, express the goal of coming with their lover inside them. "When I come with my lover's penis in my vagina," Linda said, "I am in a state of ecstasy." If you feel that way, there is nothing wrong with such a goal, and you shall have it. It has probably already occurred. If it hasn't, sex will not support an immediate goal, so forget it, and do your exercises and the processes in this chapter. You will have, by your practice together, what you want.

Sexuality is an infinite space. The variation of sexuality is amazing—there *are* no limits. How you come doesn't matter. It only matters that you know how to give yourself pleasure and communicate to others how to give you pleasure.

What's really important is that you make love to people, not sex. We all want to be knowledgeable and the best lover we can. Let's always remember, however, that we do make love to people, not to the god of sex. Every person has his or her own unique experience of orgasm. In the last analysis you don't make love to a machine, or measurements, but to another person.

CHAPTER 6

Exercises and Sexual Aids for the Advanced

Whatever your level of sexual pleasure before you began this book, I hope I have offered you a different kind of lovemaking, one defined by stillness. You learned that whenever you make love you can feel ecstasy. And if you reached that level you know you can go to higher levels. These levels call on scientific technology as well as body movements. Now I will explore with you the advanced patterns of the internal embrace, and the secrets and uses of enhancing devices. Together they create another dimension of the expression of human sexuality.

The Pleasure-Right Principle

Why, in this chapter on advanced sexual techniques, are devices included? Because science has a contribution to make to advanced knowledge of the sexual self. Sexual aids and devices are man-made objects that stimulate and intensify your sexual sensations. They come in various categories. Sexual aids enhance sensual pleasure and provide options in lovemaking. That is possible because many of the new aids are based on the latest research into female sexuality. They are used to exercise your love muscle.

Most women are afraid to buy sexual devices. Some don't even know of their existence. In fact, I use an environmental approach in my sex therapy practice—I take women to sex shops, and provide them with catalogues.

Solitary sensual exercises increase your control and generate sexuality.

Breath of Passion

1. It's important to look at yourself. Sit in front of a mirror.
2. Sit in a cross-legged position and breathe. Rest your hands palms up on your legs.
3. Exhale, hold your breath, and tighten your love muscle.
4. Now pant hard at the same time as you rapidly pulse your muscle. Feel you are sucking the juice out of a flower. Purse your lips and blow and clench repeatedly. This exercise may bring you directly to orgasm.

Soul Kissing

1. Put some delicate honey on your lips.
2. Sit cross-legged, and look in the mirror. Stick out your tongue.
3. Make a circle around your lips and lick the honey. Tense your muscle, and thrust your tongue in and out as far as it will go.
4. Keep your muscle tense. Lick as if licking an ice cream.
5. Relax.

Dancing

1. Get on all fours, and face the mirror sideways.
2. Level your back. Then arch it way up like a cat.
3. Lower your back into a swayback and stick your buttocks up and out high in the air.
4. Clench your love muscle and pulse it.
5. Pull up the perineum, pull up the anus. Experiment with that feeling.
6. Sway your back, and as you do pull up tight inside.

The Internal Embrace

When your eroticism is to be shared with a lover, exercises for the advanced are thrusting and gripping patterns. Again, think of your vagina as a tower of golden rings. Let's imagine you have six rings. Your lover moves into you to various depths of the rings.

Diving

His penis moves into you like a stone sinking slowly into the water. You press on its thick sides, pulling tighter as he pulls out. Then he thrusts slowly in again, to about the third ring, and you clench. You pause. He pulls out, and goes in again to the deepest ring, very slowly. You clench as he pulls out. He clenches to keep from coming.

The Eagle Strike

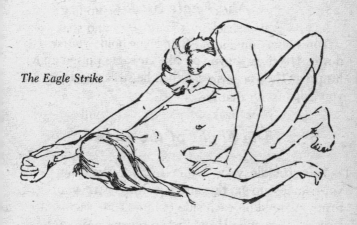

Nine and One, The Honorable Technique

This is the most treasured method of the ancient secret sexual arts of China. Your lover thrusts nine times to the middle, or third ring, then once deep into the very top. You can vary the speed. You lift your pelvis and do the slow and sustained grip. Hold him tightly as he slides nine times to the third ring and tack out to the tightness of the entrance. Then he thrusts deeply up to the very top. As he does, you grip that last final thrust high up in the rings, as in the last part of the Slow and Sustained Grip.

He goes nine times shallow, one deep, for nine times. At the tenth time, his last thrust is the deepest.

The Eagle Strike

You lie on your back. Your lover holds your wrists down. He rises above you like an eagle poised above his prey. Then he strikes. When he strikes and thrusts, you grip.

The Flight of the Dove

You straddle your lover. Hunker over him with your knees up in the air, squatting with your feet firmly planted on each side of him. Your vagina faces him. He lies still. He is just to receive. Move down over his penis, and as you ride up and down, pant and clench in the breath of passion.

The Flight of the Dove

Sexual Devices

Whenever you have an orgasm, there will be reflexive muscle contractions in your love muscle, and perhaps the uterus. These contractions, that is, orgasm, can be created not only by your voluntary contraction of the love muscle, either alone or with a partner, but by a variety of mechanical aids. In fact, this is one of the methods of choice prescribed for women who have never had had an orgasm. Contractions hasten the process.

Now that you are advanced, you can avail yourself of some of these sexual aids to add to your pleasure. I will tell you about some of them, and some of the other advanced aspects of sexuality. Devices have added technology, brought the twentieth century into the bedroom; they can double your pleasure. Sexual devices run the gamut from artificial vaginas, blow-up women, double penises, to biofeedback and electrical devices that exercise the love muscle. Some are only available on prescription. The sex business is booming, but the problem is that most of the quality is shabby and poor. It's basically a mail order business, with ads stuck in the back of magazines. However, there are some classy educational mail order houses and sex stores that serve to educate the public about sex as well as sell devices. Eve's Garden in Boston and New York, Joani Blank's Good Vibrations in San Francisco, the Xandria Collection in San Francisco, and Tex William's Sensory Research Corporation in Bloomfield, New Jersey, have the most sophisticated, enlightened view. They intend to make you feel good about your body and good about sexuality, and they care about quality. All of them have usually invented products of their own that pushed forward the frontiers of sexual knowledge and enhancement. The original vibrators were not invented by sex researchers, they were invented to make money. They started as massagers, and women began to use them all over their bodies to have orgasms from the stimulation. The newer sex businesses in the sex bazaar have created products that go beyond vibrators. These are designed to titillate all of your senses.

Sensory Delights

Love oils taste good, and are used while licking your lover during oral sex.

Massage lotions and oils heighten the enjoyment of touch. They sink into the skin, leaving a delicious odor. Some of the most advanced include a recently isolated group of chemicals of human sexuality called pheromones that attract the opposite sex like a magnet.

Perfume bases are the pure oil of a scent, such as ambergris, myrrh, civet oil, musk, frankincense. These essential oils are ancient. They have symbolic value and are used to evoke specific moods. Myrrh is accounted a purifier. Musk is used to excite sexuality, and to cast love spells. Patchouli was sacred to the god Pan. Sandalwood was used in the East for meditation. The greatest use of these oils is as aphrodisiacs.

We're only becoming aware of the powerful nature of scent messages. In humans, pheromones seem to act as they do among moths—the male moth will sense and respond to one molecule of female attractant in a hundred thousand. Eve's Garden notes that an airline scented a plane to smell like mother's milk to make all the passengers feel secure.

Sex stores and catalogues also sell a variety of items that are pleasing to the touch. I use feathers, velvet, satin, silk, wooden beads, soaps, and fur to awaken the sense of touch in workshops. A woman dusted with power on a huge puff will sometimes burst into tears, or smile with pure joy. Such sensual delights make the body feel alive. Also sold are natural sponges to use in the bath, feather dusters, fur underpants, mink mitts, wooden back massagers.

Plug-in Vibrators

The vibrator has given a lot of women orgasms. Joani Blank wrote a pioneering book, *Good Vibrations*, to demystify the subject. I recommend it. It answers any questions you might have. But she clearly states, and I agree, that all women don't have to be vibrator enthusiasts. It is also true that vibrators can be used as well with a partner.

In my opinion the best vibrators are the plug-in variety, with a cord. They come with varying degrees of vibration intensity. Some are silent, which gives you more privacy if you want to use them alone. Some come with special attachments to stimulate the clitoris, and others have attachments for overall body massage. Some have a scalp massager, or special attachments for the head of the penis.

Starting with the most quiet and least intense, here are descriptions of the more elegant devices.

A vibrator is a matter of personal choice. Every woman varies. You should test what you like. Many are now available in major department stores, such as Bloomingdale's in New York. They are most frequently used for self-stimulation, but you can use them with your partner to stimulate your love muscle, or your clitoris, or, as some have special male attachments, his penis. Some also can be used during intercourse.

1. THE PRELUDE 3 (SENSORY RESEARCH CORP., BLOOMFIELD, NJ)

This is the gentlest and quietest of all available vibrators. It has two speeds and five attachments, including a special clitoral stimulator, which looks like a kind of button. It also includes four other attachments that are very interestingly shaped. One looks like a wafflemaker. The vibrator also has a male attachment specifically designed to stimulate the head of the penis for masturbation, or play before sex. It looks like a small cup.

2. HITACHI MAGIC WAND (HITACHI CORP., JAPAN)

The Magic Wand is sold as a body massager and is great for masturbation if you prefer stronger intensity.

This is the Rolls-Royce of vibrators. It is extremely well made. It has a large, heavy, wandlike plastic body, and a round head on a flexible neck. It vibrates in two speeds of very intensely diffusing vibrations.

It also comes in a double-head model, for those who want double stimulation. It is also great for body massage!

Battery-Powered Vibrators

These are usually insertable, a little noisier, but great for traveling.

1. ORGO STIMULATOR (EVE'S GARDEN, NEW YORK AND BOSTON)

I call this the androgynous stimulator. It has a flexible gooseneck wand topped by a bullet-shaped vibrating top. It runs quietly and slips between two people who are making love, stimulating the clitoris for masturbation. Its throbbing sensation that you feel through the pubic bone gives pleasure to each partner if you hold it between you during intercourse.

One of the delights of battery-powered vibrators is that they can be inserted safely inside the body. This one is enjoyable in the vagina or the anus.

2. PHALLIC-SHAPED BATTERY-OPERATED DEVICES

They are widely available in different lengths with various raised dots for texture, and with different degrees of flexibility. The batteries fit in the bottom and are turned on by twisting the bottom cover.

These are insertable and give pleasure both vaginally and anally. The most widely known and bought vibrators, they are the least expensive. They lack nothing in quality or pleasure and are good for beginners.

Dildos

Dildos have a long history. The ancient Chinese made them out of jade, ivory, and silver. In whaling nations the penis bone of the sperm whale was highly prized. Dildos have been made out of brass, and even permanently attached to chairs. What women have wanted is to have something to press against inside them. A dildo inside your vagina feels like a penis. Other than that, there are no limitations to what makes a dildo. There are many kinds.

Some undulate or are made with curves. A dildo is controlled by you, it is not powered by batteries or electricity. In fact, it's a good way to learn the thrusting patterns or practice your love muscle exercises. Dildos come in all lengths and materials and are sold by all sex stores. You can use them to massage the end of the cervix and (indirectly) the love muscle. Your lover can manipulate one while massaging your clitoris. They are also used for anal pleasure by both sexes.

ORGANIC DILDOS

You can probably find a dildo right in your own refrigerator, an organic dildo. Use a carrot (clean it first) or a cucumber. They can be surprisingly satisfying.

Dangling Your Toes over the Edge

For those who are really adventurous there are other devices a little beyond the fringe. Did you know there are candy underpants that your lover can eat off?

OINTMENTS, BALMS, AND UNGUENTS

Rub these substances on your clitoris or on your partner's penis. They stimulate circulation, or else feel cool and numbing. An underground classic is the Chinese medicament Tiger Balm, found in any health food store or Chinese grocery. It comes in red and white. The red is hotter. It makes the clitoris feel larger. It is not edible.

FRENCH TICKLERS

These are one of a class of covers for the penis. They rub and tickle against the cervix and create a mad variety of sensations. Off the penis, they look like a collection of sea urchins. They are usually made of soft pliable plastic with various lengths of bumps, ridges or feelers.

CORONAL EXTENDERS

These are a sort of Mickey Mouse ears that fit over the end of the penis. They were designed by Dr. Kegel to stimulate the love muscle in the vagina. The ears are placed to rub against your areas of sensitivity (see clock test in sexological exam). These days they are a rare find, however, as Dr. Kegel's view that the vagina is sexually sensitive has fallen into disuse after Masters and Johnson and the rise of information on clitoral orgasm.

BEN WA BALLS AND THE STRING OF PEARLS

Ben Wa balls are an ancient Oriental device: two balls, either separate or on a string, are inserted into the vagina and held in with either muscle strength or a tampon. After they are inserted, the woman goes on about her daily business. Since ancient times, women have used them while sitting in a rocking chair and rocking back and forth for a sensation of pleasure.

The string of pearls is a string of large round beads, plastic or wooden, securely strung on a strong cord with a ring at the end. They are inserted one by one in your lover's anus during sex play or intercourse, and then rapidly pulled out all at once at the moment he reaches orgasm.

COCK RINGS

You may see ads for rings to put around your partner's penis to maintain an erection. They can have various textures or shapes and may be attached to a vibrating device that helps stimulate the penis and the clitoris during intercourse.

STRAP-ON VIBRATORS

This new form of vibrator is small and flat and straps on directly over the clitoris, with the straps going around the upper legs. It can be used during intercourse.

ANAL STIMULATORS

These are vibrators to use inside the anus. They are held on the outside and inserted. They range from pencil-thin to thick and stubby. Some also have nubs or ticklers.

BONDAGE DEVICES

Sex stores and catalogues also cater to special interests in sex. One of them is bondage, in which one partner binds or otherwise immobilizes the other. Most of these straps, collars, wrist bands, and harnesses are sold in the same areas as other sexual adjuncts. The excitement about them is that they are the means of playing out the power struggle sometimes implicit in sex. If there is a power struggle, it can be healthy to act it out safely.

Love Muscle Exercise Devices

It's become very acceptable to use devices—particularly a whole new class of them medically recommended and designed to exercise the vaginal muscles. Most such devices are based on recent scientific evidence on the importance of the love muscle. This is the fastest growing area of aids, because sex researchers have only just begun to recognize the connection between internal fitness and orgasm.

There are several such devices already on the market. The two basic types are biofeedback and electrical. Biofeedback devices indicate the strength of your love muscle by beeping or lighting up. Electrical aids contract the muscle for you by stimulating it electrically.

My point in this book is that it is exercise and not devices that will most help your sexuality. However, there are people, as physiologist Dr. John Huffman of Northwestern University points out, who are born with congenitally poor love muscles. They have no awareness of its function and cannot control it. Frequently these individuals wet the bed as children and are nonorgasmic as adults. If you cannot identify and control your muscle you need an external device to help you. And in that case, isn't science wonderful?

Early Biofeedback Devices

The first biofeedback device used to exercise the love muscle was the perineometer, invented by Dr. Kegel. It was the only aid available for thirty years, required a physician's prescription, and was used for urinary stress incontinence. Though not prescribed for orgasm, that often turned out to be its pleasant side effect. The device is a simple air-pressure gauge attached to an inflatable bulb, with an attached readout dial that the patient could hold in her hand to see the strength of a contraction. This nonelectronic biofeedback device predated biofeedback theory.

The medical profession and the sex profession largely ignored Kegel's work and his device, except in regard to urinary stress incontinence, because of the lack of wide-scale testing. Even when recent evidence overwhelmingly indicated that strengthening the love muscle leads to orgasm, Kegel's device was considered inconclusive by the scientific profession. He had offered very little objective scale by which a user could measure her strength against another's for test purposes. The results were not quantifiable. In fact, at one point, Kegel and Masters actually wound up in court testifying on opposite sides over the issue of sexual sensitivity in the vagina. What happened is not widely known. Dr. Masters admits that such a case took place, but declines comment. No exercises involving the inside of the vagina, such as I suggest,

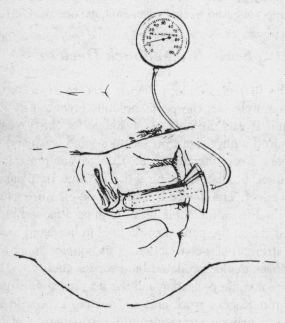

The perineometer

were ever acknowledged or suggested by Masters and Johnson.

Dr. Hungerford, a psychologist, says, "It remains a mystery why Kegel's exercises are known and practiced throughout the world for urinary stress incontinence, but the sexual findings of Kegel's work have been ignored. Certainly, he raised the old controversy about vaginal orgasms. Dr. Masters was extremely antagonistic to Kegel. There was a period of conflict between them, and I observed that all the years that I knew Dr. Kegel, Dr. Masters was very, very careful to avoid any mention of the vaginal contractions. He omitted it. I think he is responsible for all the emphasis on clitoral stimulation as the only way to orgasm—which is a bunch of nonsense."

Kegel maintained that there are sexual sense receptors on top of the love muscle. Most doctors argued, and would still, that the vagina has no nerve endings and is only sensitive to pressure, nothing else. Kegel disagreed. He invented coronal extenders to touch areas he believed were sensitive. In the court case Kegel was an expert witness defending the possibility of stimulating women vaginally. Masters denied it.

As we have seen, various important organs of female sexual anatomy are only just being acknowledged. What has been scientifically verified to date is that exercise of the vaginal muscles is imperative to the health of the muscle.

The perineometer is no longer available. I describe it at length because it was the first biofeedback device to exercise the love muscle.

The controversy continues in modern terms between those who believe in electrical stimulation to passively exercise your muscle and those who advocate biofeedback so that you can learn to exercise it yourself.

Whatever the method, it is most important that you learn to identify this unique muscle so that it is an accepted part of yourself, and you are comfortable using it.

Advanced Biofeedback Devices

Researcher and biofeedback expert John Perry, rediscoverer with Whipple of the Gräfenberg spot, is a prime advocate of the uses of technology in sex. (The Gräfenberg spot was first described in 1950 by Dr. E. Gräfenberg, whose work was only resurrected when Perry and Whipple searched for previous references to a spot of sensitivity in the vagina.) Perry invented the vaginal myograph, which probes and measures cervical contractions during orgasm. Currently he is working on a home biofeedback model for vaginal exercise which will have lights that blink on and off, and perhaps even a graph readout of levels of contraction.

Perry's research indicates that women can definitely learn to clench their muscles and hold the clench for longer periods when a sound or light is kept going to alert them to when they are contracting. He also believes learning to relax the muscle is of great importance. His devices are the latest in the measurement of female sexual response. Their aim is to teach you how to control your own muscle.

There are other, less elaborate biofeedback devices currently on the market, but unfortunately they are also rather inadequate. There is one called the PC Muscle Trainer, which looks like a large thermometer. You are supposed to be able to see the level reached by the red fluid. However, the bulb you insert is too short, and the liquid doesn't go up the tube. Another is a glorified dildo and is not effective. All of them are therapeutic in nature, and are used for people who have health or sex problems. For this book, we are not coming from a problem-oriented position in sex. This is a book about pleasure, and my main interest in these aids is how they may be used to increase your pleasure.

Electrical Stimulators of the Love Muscle

This class of devices are inserted into the vagina and emit a barely discernible electrical current at regular intervals directly onto the vaginal muscles to contract them. Muscles work electrically. If you stimulate them with a small amount of electrical current they automatically contract. This is a trick of first-year biology classes—the isolated muscle of a frog's leg is stimulated with an electrode so it contracts as though the frog were jumping.

THE VAGITONE (TECHNI-MED, WHITTIER, CA)

This is the best device; it was invented by general practitioner Dr. Roger Foster. It has been tested and is advocated by Dr. Edwin Rudinger, a fellow of the

American College of Gynecology. Dr. Rudinger has had three cases of interest recently. "All 3 patients were in their early 20's and all 3 were suffering from primary anorgasmia [they had never had an orgasm]. Also, all three could not contract their PC muscle, even after very careful instructions on how to do this they had no objective ability to contract the muscle. I put each on the vagitone and two . . . were able to have their first orgasm with intercourse in three and four days respectively. The third patient was able to have an orgasm after two and one-half weeks. All three . . . when rechecked were voluntarily able to contract their PC muscle with ease. They were very grateful and couldn't believe the fantastic results in so short a time."

The Vagitone is available only by prescription. The Vagitone works to exercise the muscle. It is battery-powered, but doesn't vibrate. It is shaped something like a pistol. The surface is silicon rubber, with a warm esthetic "feel." You hold it by the pistol grip, which has an intensity dial on its end. The insert (or barrel) has two conductive bands embedded about a centimeter apart on the end. It emits a pleasant tingling pulse every two seconds, which make the internal muscle contract.

I personally think it's the finest instrument available to use for pleasure in coordination with doing your love muscle exercises.

You can use it while lying in bed at night, while you watch TV, relaxing and feeling the delightful internal stimulation. It has an automatic eleven-minute shut off for safety.

THE VAGETTE (MYODYNAMICS, CARSON, CA)

Dr. Robert Scott, clinical professor of obstetrics and gynecology at USC, has popularized the use of a vaginal exerciser that is a variation on the Vagitone but is available without prescription. The Vagette is less expensive and does not have a calibration on the knob that controls the intensity of electrical stimulation.

I don't like the plastic of which it is made, and changing the batteries can be difficult. Dr. Scott's clinical trials have shown, however, that it does increase vaginal pleasure.

For maximum effect, I would recommend doing the exercises while having your love muscle electrically stimulated.

New Entries

The idea of exercising the interior vaginal muscles has already spawned new entries into what promises to be a lucrative field. One example is a device made from a simple knobbed bar of brass. Its inventor, Stuart Bloch of Montclair, New Jersey, claims that the differential in temperature between the body and the colder solid metal will automatically cause the muscle to contract without electrical stimulation.

There is no way of evaluating such claims, nor have any studies on it as yet been released. I can only point out that there are bound to be many more items soon in the sex bazaar. What the brass device does do, in some opinions, is feel good, vaginally or anally, and so it has started to be used for sexual pleasure.

There are some new devices currently being developed specifically to stimulate the Gräfenberg spot, but they are not on the market yet.

Pleasures of the Mind: Erotica

Sex is in the mind. Erotica is a major way to appeal to the mind as well as the body. The trouble has been that it was never available to women. Women were told repeatedly (by Kinsey, for example) that they did not respond to the sight of a maked male. Males, however, were free to buy and enjoy every aspect of erotica.

However, the classic arousal studies done by Julia Heiman showed that men and women exhibit equal erotic potential when exposed to erotica. The measuring devices recorded arousal changes, but the women didn't report them to the researchers. Masters and Johnson, in their famous *Playboy* interview, maintained that given the chance, women will react to male nudity much as males do to female nudity. Masters and Johnson felt that pornography gained its excitement from being forbidden.

Women are socialized to repress signs of sexual arousal. That is why this book focuses so much on autoeroticism. As your guide to sensual pleasure, I want to lead you into erotica. Erotica implies a "healthy" interest in arousal. People are turned on by seeing other people naked and seeing them make love, and by reading about sex. Erotica has been a tool to enhance pleasure throughout time. Many famous artists from Toulouse-Lautrec to Picasso have created largely repressed portfolios of erotica. Erotica has been more accepted in the upper classes of Western culture, in France, Holland, and England. Famed artists of erotica were often attached to royal houses. Most erotica is still kept in private collections.

In our culture a lot of erotica and pornography is carried in magazines. Women feel funny buying it, however, and the shops that carry it are off limits for a lot of women.

So far, the scientific literature shows that many women like explicit scenes of sexuality to read or look at.

Perhaps, too, you might like to hear erotic stories. There are lovers who whisper erotic stories in your ear. We've been speaking all along about the differences in orgasm. And there is a big difference in sex, also. There are all kinds of sex: low, high, funky, horny, boring. In some of these, pornography plays its role.

The boom in videotapes and X-rated movies is due in part to the fact that these mediums give women the safety to enjoy pornography in the home—and use it for fun. Unfortunately, some of this material is exploitive, and gives financial support to people who profit from that exploitation. It can distort one's ability to experience a truly sensual sense of pleasure, because it convolutes sexuality and uses people for the worst reasons. Pornography at its best is erotica. Pornography shows you kinds of sexuality other than your own. In workshop surveys I examined women's attitudes toward pornography. The majority of women said they enjoyed a wide variety of pornography, both visual and written.

Fantasy Fun

Fantasy can be great fun. You can share it, whisper it in your lover's ear, make up stories together—and you don't have to act on it.

Take your hot bonds to bed with you. Using fantasy is part of an advanced repertoire of sexual techniques to reach orgasm with a partner. As a matter of fact, people with orgasmic problems are regularly taught to use fantasy while making love. Some people feel that putting their mind on some delightful fantasy will be betraying their lover, but these are *your* enhancements; they can relax and excite you, they can be used to turn you on, or turn your lover on. In a workshop, Viv said, "I put my mind on whatever I want to when I think of coming." Fantasy is fun and your bedroom is your playroom.

Fantasy is a major component of sex. In my experience, virtually everybody fantasizes during intercourse at some time or another. So, it is okay to have fantasies—there is nothing wrong with any fantasy. The content of a fantasy is irrelevant. If you don't feel guilty about it afterward, or, if it is violent in nature, as long as you don't actually do it, a fantasy is perfectly healthy.

To fantasize is, in a sense, to step into your greatest desires and fears. It can be used to free you from fear, for example, by helping you feel more comfortable with what frightens you. Fantasy can also be a clue to what you most want.

When people try to act out their fantasies, they are often very disappointed. When they cross the line from imagination to the real world the fantasy loses its delight. Why? So many variables are introduced by reality that you can no longer control the fantasy. You have to react to real people. The essence of fantasy is that you are in control of all the conditions.

How to Use Fantasy in Intercourse

It is very exciting to use an erogenous fantasy in intercourse. There's nothing wrong with it, and it need not be shared with your partner. But if you do want to share your fantasy with your lover you can create a word picture and whisper it in his ear as you are making love. This can be a great turn-on and can create extreme intimacy between you. When both of you are trusting and share your fantasy, it can create a sense of warmth.

You can also use fantasy specifically to create excitement while you are making love, particularly if you know what turns your lover on. You can observe him, or ask his favorites. If he is like most men he may respond to some common fantasies. Your communication to him can then be an aphrodisiac.

Fantasy can be a healthy way to express a person's need to be dominated, and to help the person get aroused. In our culture, seven out of ten women and eight out of ten men have fantasies in which they are *dominated*. In my practice I have noticed that most people's fantasy is that they are being ruled by others. Surprisingly for some women, men, particularly men in powerful positions, like to fantasize being dominated.

The idea of domination is tied to that of bondage. Fantasies of bondage and domination are a release valve for anger, in which aggression can be expressed positively. They can also be shared as you both get aroused, as long as you are not hurting anyone in reality.

Forbidden Fruit

The most common fantasy for a man is having sex with two women. The most common fantasies for women are being overpowered by a man, having sex with a group, or making love to another woman.

Here are some real women's fantasies:

Being the center of attention of several males (whom I know and like very much). Having them all treating me gently, as a princess, pampering me, stimulating me, kissing me, having sex with all of them.

I would like to be asleep in my own bed at home, and I would like to be awakened by my lover. He would not be alone; he would bring me a surprise, another woman.

I go to a magic garden, with beautiful flowers and winding paths like a maze, with a pool in the center. This pool has rosewater and milk in it. I take off my dirty jeans and step into the pool. Men come to serve me, they bathe me, feed me, wait on me. The slender one makes love to me.

My biggest fantasy is watching two men have sex while I make love.

I lie in a bed in a darkened room, and a man comes in and makes love to me.

I'm standing in front of an audience of men naked except for masks. One by one I choose the men to kneel at my feet and eat me.

I lie naked on a table surrounded by men dressed in business suits. It's a boardroom. The door is locked. As I writhe they moan and bring their penises out. They stand up to stroke themselves over me. I look at them. They can't help themselves. They are driven to ecstasy.

Your own fantasies, whether you have done them, would want to, or would never want to, can be another arousing form of pleasure during lovemaking. Feel free to use it.

Fantasy in Reality

Because so many men and women have similar erotic fantasies, it's quite common to act them out, and you can do that in your playroom. Surveys of women's fantasies show the wish to try some form of bondage and domination, sex with another woman, group sex, or anal sex. Most men express fantasies of group sex or a menage a trois, oral sex, domination, and anal sex.

BONDAGE

This is a struggle-and-surrender play. The silken side of bondage is acting out a fantasy with your lover, where you tie him up with ribbons, or he lightly "ties" you with scarves. You can begin a game of struggle, in which you try to capture the other person. The point is to struggle and wrestle.

You can also use heavier leather such as that available at sex bazaars. You can also go to surgical-supply houses. There you can get restraints, usually comfortable and in white or other soft colors, covered with lambswool at chafing points, used for hospital patients.

ANAL SEX

Moré and more men express the wish to have anal sex with women. One reason may be that it's almost a virginal area for many women, something new. Most women are reluctant, however, mainly because they can't relax their anal muscles. (The exercises for tensing and relaxing your love muscle are helpful for this. They help you focus on opening and relaxing that muscle, if you want to experience it. Love muscle exercises and gripping patterns are delightfully effective in anal sex.) If you do want to have sex in this way, it is essential that the man penetrate slowly and with attention, and that you use lubrication.

EXHIBITIONISM AND VOYEURISM

There is a lighter side to what we usually think of as criminal activities. In these games with your lover, you are the one being watched during sexual acts, or you watch your lover. You can elaborate this in fantasy, or do it in real life. We're all voyeurs at sex films, for example, and we all look at each other. Some people get a lot of enjoyment out of the fantasy of exhibiting themselves masturbating, or of having sex while other people watch, or of being one of the watchers.

ADS

Often people run ads to get a sexual partner or meet people who have similar fantasies to act out.

IN THE PLAYROOM

You can enjoy playing in your bedroom. Do you want to dress up? Go ahead. Some people like to pretend they are animals together. They menace each other with growls, and spring. Certain sounds evoke emotional states, and you may enjoy humming, or humming together. Some noises can soothe, such as a constant voice talking, murmuring to you. Your voice or your lover's can act like white noise and block out distractions.

Biting and scratching are also time-honored in lovemaking, the muscles at the base of the neck being particularly sensitive to biting. It's normal for men and women to want to emit sounds when they have an orgasm. You can experiment with that, let yourself go.

You can use fantasy and play even when you are

separated, such as setting a time when both of you will masturbate while thinking of each other, then telling each other about it over the phone the next day. You can masturbate together on the phone.

Games and fantasy are so powerful that in some cities now there are services that work by credit card; they put a person of the sex you want on the phone with whatever fantasy you want. They promise to continue fantasizing until you come.

Feeding Your Lover

Studies at the State University of New York show that people who enjoy food usually enjoy sex. It doesn't matter how *much* you eat, just how much you enjoy it. Food and sex have always been linked, since Aphrodite was the goddess of both love and crops.

Some substances have been isolated and reported as aphrodisiacs, but what seems to be more pertinent is the look and feel of the food. Some foods arouse psychosexual images, and it is those foods we want to suggest you feed your lover.

Arrange on a tray foods that are easily eaten by hand, or in raw form. They should be of the highest quality. Put out raw oysters and clams, asparagus with hollandaise sauce; tiny slivers of avocado, cherry tomatoes; fruits, large chunks of melon, berries to dip in sugar or sour cream, cherries, some cheese, nuts. Just small amounts, nothing weighted down.

Then offer some favorite chocolates, a sweet tart, ice cream bonbons.

The main thing is that it be beautifully presented, and that you can pick it up and feed each other.

Other Play

When the play-acting is creative, there are all manner of sensual experiences that can lead up to sexual intercourse. If you have the talent or inclination, you can make drawings of each other's genitals or bodies, or mold them. There are body paints for lovers, and paint tattoos and designs to try, as well as glitter lotion and body glitter.

Your sexual behavior is an expression of your humanness. The tremendous range of woman's sensuality, and your right to explore it, should be clear to you by now.

CHAPTER 7

Sex, Health, and Fitness

Studies show that people who are fit are generally more interested in sex, and are having more sex. For a long time, women in sports suffered from the general idea that athletic women were probably asexual. Chris Evert says, "Just fifteen years ago, a woman athlete wasn't a normal human being: she was a freak. Now we are looked up to."

Hartman and Fithian have documented that joggers and others in fit condition have easy orgasm, less physiologically stressful and no less intense than those of nonathletically active women.

Up to 17 million adults are now running or jogging regularly in this country. Seventy-three percent more women have taken up sports over the last two years than did in the previous year. Thirty to fifty percent of women report that they do at-least an hour's exercise per day. The fitness revolution is here. The reason is that we have all come to recognize the pressures of twentieth-century living, and the preventive necessity of exercise. You can see why women who exercise simply feel more sexual—they use their bodies, gain respect for them, and must "listen" to them—all conducive to a good sexual self-image. Hardness and firmness, and respect for your own regular exercise program, can increase sexual self-esteem. There are actual physical changes in the body from extended aerobic exercise, including increased cardiovascular circulation, which makes sex much more pleasurable; increased blood flow to the muscles, which is necessary for feeling sensory input, especially in such activities as aerobic dancing or adult ballet; specialized body movements that increase flexibility and strengthen the body for sex. But what we all didn't know, and all should know, is that fitness must include *interior* muscles as well. Women (and men) have known about pelvic problems for thousands of years, but treating them was difficult, as they were essentially hidden. The gynecological textbook of the Roman physician Soranus (110 A.D.) was still in use into the 1800s. The vagina was always considered mysterious. When doctors did start studying the physiology of muscles after World War II, they ignored women's internal muscles. Dr. Kegel felt that was due in part to the fact that doctors had begun using anesthesia routinely in childbirth, and so never saw these muscles working. It is also a fact that muscles are learned about through dissection, and the dissection process cannot show contractibil-

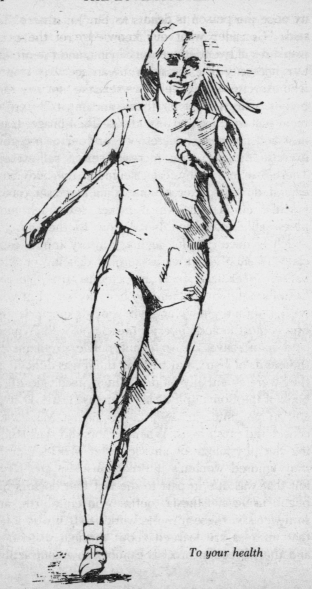

To your health

ity once the person is dead. (As Dr. Jonathan Miller said, "Consider what our knowledge of the penis would be if we only knew it from dissection.") The love muscle wasn't considered a contractible muscle under *voluntary* control. Physiologists believe that pelvic muscles are the ones that used to wag the tail, when our ancestors were on all fours. That provided automatic exercise, which we lost when we lost our tail. Because we are not taught early in life to exercise this muscle (and some people are born with it already weak), there is an increasing incidence of all the annoying, and expensive "female" problems.

Preventive Health

Keeping sexually fit has a vital preventive health function. Over eighteen conditions that are painfully annoying, leading to expensive medicine or surgery, can be prevented or cured by your love muscle exercises. As you age, gravity pulls the muscle downward. The love muscle should ideally be a straight line, but, because it supports all of your internal organs, it tends to sag. If it is congenitally weak or has been damaged at childbirth, which is very common, and you do not do love muscle exercises, you will have some of these conditions.

One early study examined four-thousand nursing students who had never had children and found that 52 percent of them already had some degree of loss of urine with stress, indicating inherent weakness in the love muscle.

Conditions that can often be cured or prevented by love muscle exercise include urinary stress incontinence; painful intercourse; lack of orgasm; pelvic pain; chronic vaginitis; chronic cystitis; frequent urination; menstrual cramps; difficult childbirth making episiotomy a necessity; hysterectomy; bulges into the vaginal barrel from the rectum (rectocele); bulges from the bladder into the vagina (cystocele); or prolapse of the uterus (in which the uterus falls outside or protrudes into the vagina). Most of these conditions can be helped only minimally by any form of exercise except that directed specifically at the love muscle.

Common Problems and Conditions Prevented by Love Muscle Exercises

Condition	Symptoms
General	
Chronic vaginitis	Persistent itching, vaginal irritation, discharge.
Chronic cystitis	Persistent irritation of the urinary tract and bladder.
Urinary stress incontinence	Seepage of urine under stress.
Urge incontinence	Overfrequent urination.
Nocturina	Frequent urination during the night.
Enuresis	Wetting the bed.

Condition	Symptoms
Conditions treated by surgery	
Prolapse of the uterus }hysterectomy	Womb falling into the vagina or protruding outside.
Fibroid tumors	Benign tumors, bleeding.
Rectocele	Bulges in the vagina from the rectum.
Cystocele	Bladder protrudes into the vagina.
Urethrocele	Urethra bulges into the vagina (swelling).
Painful menstruation	Cramps, pelvic pain, and so forth.
Chronic back pain	Heavy, aching generalized pain in the lower spine.
Constipation	Lack of tone in lower intestines, difficulty in elimination.
Weakness of abdominal muscles	Bulging stomach, swayback, back pain.
Sexual problems	
Lack of orgasm (lack of orgasm in intercourse, difficulty in attaining orgasm)	Irritability, reduced quality of life, lack of sleep, emotional upset.
Vaginismus	Penis unable to penetrate vagina, due mostly to clamping of the vagina.
Painful intercourse	Penile entry painful, thrusting hurts.
Diaphragm uncomfortable	Diaphragm is felt by partner during intercourse, feels uncomfortable. Lower

Condition	Symptoms
	back pain (exercise reduces size of diaphragm used).
Birthing issues	
Infertility	Trouble getting pregnant (exercises help by increasing circulation).
Pregnancy	Exercises prior to conception and during pregnancy lessen birth trauma.
Birthing	Strong love muscles make for easier delivery with less damage to pelvic muscles and surrounding tissue.
Episiotomy	Cut to widen vaginal opening during delivery. Healthy muscle reduces need for this.
Postpartum tone	Exercises restore tone and strength of pelvic floor, encourage rapid recovery, and help restore size of vaginal canal without surgery.

You Can Choose Exercise, Not Surgery

The treatment of choice (meaning of the doctor's choice) for most problems in a woman's pelvic area is surgery. That was true when Kegel first invented internal exercises, and it is still true today. For one condition, urinary stress incontinence, his exercises are just what the doctor ordered, but the trouble is that most women do not do them past the two weeks needed to bring about the first results.

Why? Consider the profit in surgery, and the numbers of unnecessary pelvic operations. Another reason is that the exercises indisputably make women feel aroused. They increase sexual sensation and bring on intensified and increased orgasm. As scientists discovered when they studied training for alpha brain waves in biofeedback, what you believe about a feeling dictates how it feels to you. In an experiment that indentified subjects' alpha waves with a beeping sound, when subjects were told that the waves they were about to feel were pleasant, they reported them after the experiment as soothing and relaxing. When subjects were told they would feel nothing during alpha waves, they reported their experience as distinctly unpleasant.

When women were told only that doing vaginal exercises was necessary after giving birth to restore organs to their original shape, or to prevent urinary weakness, the other feelings in their pelvis felt "uncomfortable." In fact, they seemed inappropriately sexual. This was also the era of the frozen pelvis. They weren't supposed to feel anything "down there." When they did, women almost uniformly dropped the exercises.

When increased sensuality and delight in sex is not acknowledged as a desirable side effect, women stop doing the exercises. Since it often takes several weeks for the benefits of doing these exercises to become unmistakable, many women lost incentive. If the muscle was weak, it may also have been hard for them to identify it. That is why it is important for you to return to the urine test periodically to be certain you are using only your love muscle and not any other muscle groups as well. If you take sexuality as well as health as your goal, and you know the wonderful sensations to expect—and you accept them— then sex is healthy and health sexy.

Hysterectomies—An Ounce of Prevention

Most hysterectomies (the complete or partial removal of internal female organs) are done for pelvic relaxation (or prolapse) or benign fibroid tumors, not for cancer as many people assume. Uterine prolapse, the chief cause of hysterectomies, can be helped or eliminated by the exercises in this book. So can fibroid tumors. Prolapses usually occur after several childbirths, or with a congenitally weak love muscle. Some are so bad that the uterus actually hangs painfully out of the vagina. Hysterectomies are almost the most commonly performed operation in America today, surpassed only by the "D & C's" (dilatation and curettage) used in abortion. Even without the new love muscle information, it is clear that many of these major surgical procedures are unnecessary. In *Men Who Control Women's Health,* Diana Scully quotes a survey by Canadian researchers that found the average rate of unjustified hysterectomies for all hospitals studied was 23.7 percent and rising; in one it was as high as 59 percent. Scully also reports that the number of hysterectomies performed for insured women is double that for uninsured. There is much evidence that hysterectomies can cause a high incidence of complications and death; in 1965, 780,000 were performed, with 1,700 deaths. Cornell University Medical School's study of that year, quoted by Scully, estimated that 22 percent of these hysterectomies were unnecessary.

The uterus is involved in all phases of orgasm. Perry and others have measured uterine contractions during orgasm. When conditions are life-threatening, hysterectomies must be performed—for cancer of the uterus or cervix, excessive bleeding, other diseases of uterus or tubes, or complications of childbirth. Otherwise, you can forestall the need for surgery by setting up a program of vaginal exercise of your love muscle. Work up to at least three hundred clenches per day. Try to exercise for twenty minutes three times a day if the condition has already begun. You will only see visible results after three weeks or so but enjoy the delights of sensuality that are immediately obtainable, and *keep on*.

The women's movement has been very active in trying to prevent unnecessary hysterectomies, joined by enlightened physicians. To all of you, I urge you to turn your attention to the love muscle program as a preventive health measure.

Easing Pregnancy, Birth, and Postpartum Recovery

If you are planning to conceive, start doing these exercises now. They increase blood flow to the uterus. You want that muscle to be really strong before you start putting on weight. If you are pregnant, the exercises will be beneficial. (You might want to check with your doctor for any contraindications, however.) In Sweden, before and after a woman has a baby, a special physical therapist is brought into the room to give special pelvic floor exercises. "If you start exercises while you are pregnant," says gynecologist Dr. Robert Scott, an assistant professor of obstetrics and gynecology at USC, "it will help minimize the damage and insure you have a good recovery after delivery."

How often is your love muscle damaged in birth? Says Dr. Scott. "If it is a weak muscle? Always. One hundred percent."

Because the child's head can tear the perineal and vaginal muscles as well as the love muscle, an episiotomy, an incision at the opening of the vagina, is often done to prevent a jagged tear, which will heal badly. Is an episiotomy always necessary? Not if the woman has good muscles. Does it always damage the pelvic muscles? Says Dr. Roger Foster, developer of the Vagitone, "That depends on where it's done, how deep and what is done afterwards, and if the woman has good muscles."

Even with an episiotomy, if you can get that pelvic floor back up and bring lots of blood and oxygen to the area, you will recover faster. According to Kegel, "To no group of muscles in the human body are the general principles of muscle- and nerve-cell regeneration more applicable than to those injured in childbirth."

Doctors and Sex

Sex education was not introduced into medical schools until 1964, and even today, although most women turn for sexual advice to their general practitioner or obstetrician/gynecologist, most physicians are almost entirely untrained in female sexuality. They may not know that urinary stress exercises cause sexual arousal and may not want to mention it if they do know. Dr. Foster says, "They just don't want to listen to it, or take the time to teach a woman to exercise. As for sex—'I know a book you can read.' A lot of it is their lack of knowledge of the sexual function of the human being." They are not equipped to handle for you what I have covered in this book, because that is not their specialty.

Much of this information is very new. The information about the Gräfenberg spot, for example, has aroused some uncomfortable feelings in the profession. A senior physician in gynecology at Einstein Medical College stated that he would be quite uncomfortable and we would not like it if a woman showed signs of sexual pleasure when the Gräfenberg spot was touched during an examination. These inhibitions are genuine problems and will have to be overcome by further research and badly needed changes in the examination procedures.

Chronic Vaginal Infections

This is another area of expensive medical care for women. The itching, burning, and urinary urgency of chronic vaginitis and cystitis are usually treated by various courses of drugs containing sulfa, which some women say increases itching. These recurrent infections are caused by bacteria that normally live in the little folds and valleys of the vagina and don't bother anybody. Then for reasons known best to themselves, they become overactive and cause vaginal discharge and infection in the urinary tract. These infections can be extremely uncomfortable and are sometimes accompanied by fever.

The problem is that they are very hard to cure. There are women who have been on courses of antibiotics of various kinds to cure vaginal infections for five to ten years. The drugs have side effects and lose their effectiveness, and the infections become chronic. Urinary tract infections can lead to surgery.

Recent evidence suggests that there are preventive steps available and advocated by most physicians if the infection has not become too serious. At the first sign of urinary urgency, itching and uncomfortableness, see your doctor. It also helps to stop all stimulants, such as coffee, tea, or sodas containing caffeine, and avoid foods that are highly spiced. Gynecologist Dr. John Kerner says, "Begin drinking quantities of water to dilute any irritants to the bladder and urinary tract, and rest." Many physicians also recommended forcing (drinking quantities of) cranberry juice, which is a specific for the urinary tract.

Love muscle exercises put a stop to the vicious cycle, by inundating the area with blood and oxygen and allowing the local cells to fight the infection.

Bedwetting

Dr. Rudinger, a graduate of Columbia University's College of Physicians and Surgeons, taught a patient pelvic exercises for her own use. Her daughter, who was six, was wetting the bed. She taught her daughter to pull up the muscle, and within three weeks, the child wasn't wetting the bed anymore. Some children with congenitally weak muscles can be helped by these exercises, as can adults suffering from similar problems.

Other Surgical Conditions Preventable by Love Muscle Exercise

The love muscle exercise program, especially as outlined in "Hysterectomies—An Ounce of Prevention," will also prevent or alleviate several other conditions:

Perineal relaxation.

Bulging of the urethra (urethrocele).

Bulging of the rectum (rectocele), which causes inability to have a normal bowel movement because of a herniation or pouching of the colon into the vagina. (This frequently requires the assistance of one or two fingers introduced into the vagina to push on the pouched colon, forcing the stool out through the rectum.)

Prolapsed bladder.

Urinary incontinence.

Vaginal relaxation (for which doctors do an "A & P," a tying together of the muscles anterior and posterior, or a vaginal tuck).

Before and after unavoidable pelvic surgery.

What Dr. Kegel long ago discovered was that he had to do the same operations over and over again. "Every physician," he wrote, "has observed that six months after a well-performed vaginal repair with construction of a tight, long vaginal canal, the tissues, especially the perineum, will again become thin and weak." He soon focused on the extreme success of exercise as a preventive measure—which if maintained, did *not* reverse and was a positive cure.

This is because of the way muscle tissue functions when it is injured. Picture your body; press your fingers firmly into the muscle of your forearm until you feel the bone to which the muscle is attached. What you are feeling is not only your forearm muscle and bone but connective tissue, called fascia. It is this tissue that joins the muscle to the bone. This connective tissue is found wherever there are muscles in the body. If this tissue is torn by overstretching (or example in the vagina and uterus at childbirth), it can be surgically repaired and reattached to the bone from which it has been separated. Many doctors believed that this surgical procedure was all that was needed to repair damaged muscles.

What Kegel discovered was that these operations were doomed to failure because the muscles that had been reconnected to the bone did not regain their original strength. Only exercise can actually repair muscle. Kegel found that no matter how badly nerves were damaged in childbirth, if there were even only one or two strands still left attached, they could regenerate up to 80 percent of their function with exercise. If you know the muscles and how to contract them before the trauma, the muscle memory, will remain. It's just like riding a bicycle.

A Cure for Painful Intercourse

Several sexual problems are directly cured by exercise and keeping a high level of maintenance.

The love muscle program is recommended for people who have no orgasm, or no orgasm with intercourse, or difficulty in achieving orgasm. The program will also alleviate painful menstruation: there is evidence that weakened muscles can add to menstrual sensations of fullness and pressure. There is also a study that suggests that dysmenhorrhea (severe menstrual pain) can be helped by relaxation of the pelvic muscle, to avoid pelvic tensing after the first bad cramp. When women have pain as well in intercourse, they are in constant spasm, and the exercises are most important to relieve chronic tension.

Delaying Aging

Menopausal women can be helped by these exercises. In old age there are only two reasons why you can't have sex, right up through your eighties:

Your general physical condition

Finding a willing partner

An increase or continuation of sexual activity prevents senile vaginitis or atrophy of the vagina. Sex in old age, combined with love muscle exercises, continues lubrication. One researcher remarked that as far as she's concerned, "Sex is just as good as hormonal replacement."

Chronic Back Pain Helped

Chronic back pain, especially in the lower spine, can be helped by straightening and strengthening the lower body muscles internally. Love muscle exercises will have an aligning effect, and pull up weak abdominal muscles. They tighten and firm the stomach, keeping the internal organs in place. This can relieve some of the support pressure put on the sway of the lower back, which is often a weak and stressed part of the body. (But check any back pains with your doctor.)

Another side effect of your love muscle exercise program is that it alleviates constipation. Drs. Kenneth and Mildred Cooper, advocates of adult aerobic fitness, especially running, says, "There are no constipated runners." I'd like to add that anybody *they* missed will be helped by love muscle exercise, because it lifts the internal organs, toning the lower intestines to help elimination.

Your Fitness: What Every Woman Should Know About Running

Some general fitness exercises may be weakening if they are done without being combined with love muscle exercises. There is a controversy now brewing about women and running. Ranged on opposite sides are sports physiologists, gynecologists, and runners. The controversy is about some evidence that running can be harmful to women.

Running is one of the most popular fitness activities for women in the country. Women have become increasingly visible in marathons and smaller local distance races. The woman who runs a mile or more a day is no longer an unusual sight. Running makes us aware we are doing something wonderful for our bodies and our psyches.

However, there have been reports from sports doctors at the University of California of irregular or stopped periods in runners, and complaints about breasts sagging or hurting. Gynecologist Dr. Allan Charles, at Chicago's Michael Reese Medical Center, voiced one side when he said, "Women are not built for jogging. The uterus is not well enough supported to withstand the repeated impact caused by heels striking the ground." He advised women who experience uterine prolapse or urinary stress incontinence to stop jogging.

Dr. Mary Hungerford, who helped Kegel develop his exercises, also believes there are hazards, "unless a woman has a very strong muscle. If you're going to jog, you need to do vaginal contractions."

Evidence mounts that jogging causes excess stress on uterine muscles already in a weakened condition. Therefore, it is important that before you begin or continue running, you take the urine test and get a good idea of how strong your muscle is. Begin combined love muscle exercises as described in the following section on exercise.

Joggers must also wear strong, firmly cupped bras. If you have heavy breasts, some of the very stretchy bras can let too much bouncing occur. You can risk stretching breast muscles (unless you are following a chest exercise or weight-training program) or get what doctors call "joggers nipples." This is a problem caused by repeated irritation of the nipples.

Any reason to give up running? Unless your doctor feels it is necessary to do so for health reasons, there are many preventive health reasons to keep it up. Running resembles sex in that both release a natural analgesic, the endorphins, into the bloodstream, as well as enhance hormone secretions. James Fixx, in his wonderful book *The Complete Book of Running,* says, "Another benefit of getting into shape through running is that the pleasure of sex, for both men and women, is invariably heightened. The reason isn't mysterious. Being in good physical condition involves not just the muscles, the heart and the lungs, but all the senses as well. Runners are more aware of themselves and of others and are able to participate more fully in all aspects of life, including the sexual."

Combining Love Muscle Exercises with Fitness

I have talked about love muscle exercises throughout this book purely for their sexual pleasure. But now I want to point out the fitness side. Put another way, *not* exercising your love muscle can be injurious to your health. In order to prevent internal injury and to improve existing conditions in the pelvis, combine your love muscle exercises with your favorite sport.

For those of you who are hopeless duffers and wouldn't be caught dead working out but who walk or dance, or even just sit around, doing your love muscle exercises will cure or prevent the conditions I have mentioned.

If you *are* involved in sports and fitness, here is how to combine your exercises with several of the most popular fitness activities for maximum insurance value and strength.

Turn directly to *your* sport for the exercises you need.

Running

WARM-UPS

As you begin your first stretches to warm up, concentrate on warming up your love muscle as well.

1. Stretch up toward the ceiling or sky with both shoulders relaxed, first one arm then the other. Lift and stretch. Feel the stretch in your waist. Do this for ten times, then lower arms. Repeat the motion again, clenching your muscle every time you alternate an arm. × 10

2. Stretch your arms out at shoulder length first to one side and then to the other, moving the waist and lower back over toward the side each time. Each time you move to the side clench and release your love muscle. × 10

3. Place arms ahead of you, bend lightly from the waist, and keeping back parallel to the floor, stretch forward. Clench your muscle. Then bend with arm over head from the waist to the right side, with hands on hips to the back (gently), then with arm over the head to the left and return to front. Make the circle again clenching at each position, and reverse. × 5

4. Spread legs and pull up stomach as you bend to touch your ankles. Grasp your right ankle if possible (otherwise the calf) and pull your body down in a gentle bounce. Clench your muscle with each bounce. Feel the pull in the calf. Move to the right ankle and repeat. × 10

5. Place one foot a full step ahead of the other and

bend slowly down until you feel a distinct pull in the back leg. Grasp the front ankle. Pull and feel the stretch in your back, and clench your muscle with each light bounce.

In that position lift the toes of the front foot off the ground and lower your head to the knee if possible. Feel the good stretch in the front calf. Reverse legs and repeat.

6. Stand on the edge of a curb or stair facing it with your heels hanging over and alternately rise up on your toes and lower your heels below the level of the stair or curb. Feel the stretch in calves and Achilles tendon.

7. Sitting on the floor with your legs spread wide, try to keep the knees straight and the toes pointed. Lean over the knee on the right, grasping for the ankle, forward to put your body as close to flat as possible to a count of ten in each position. Alternate. Then repeat with the slow and sustained grip.

8. Rise and shake each of your legs as though shaking water off them. Lower your head and roll it slowly to the right, around to the back, to the left and back to the front. Reverse. Now you're ready to start your run. (Please add any other warm-up exercises you are accustomed to doing, but omit any exercises that call for a squat or sudden jerk at the knee.)

EXERCISE WHILE RUNNING

As you jog, begin with your customary slow start until you settle into a rhythm. Let your breathing settle down too, until you feel you are at a good steady pace. I hope you are running on grass; this minimizes shocks. Since that is impossible for many runners, make sure your shoes are very well padded on the heel (see *Running*). Clenching your love muscle can be combined with the rocking of your pelvis with a little practice. Don't try to do any complicated patterns, just pull up and release. A pattern that works well is to clench tight with every or every other heelstrike. Do this for at least ten minutes of your run, preferably ten minutes out of every half hour. If you are following an interval pattern, stop doing the love muscle exercises when you begin to speed up, or begin sprints.

Aerobic Dancing

Be sure you're wearing a good gym shoe, and land in all jumps with your whole foot down, not just the toes. You have your usual routine, probably, involving a warm-up on the floor.

WARM-UP

Add the following exercises to your routine:

1. Butterfly. Sit on the floor with your knees out and the heels together. Keep your back straight and grasp the ankles. Push knees apart and down toward the floor as you push your back forward from the waist. Bounce forward ten times. Then bounce the knees and thighs in a butterfly motion until they touch the floor if possible. × 10. Pull the ankles closer to the crotch, straighten back (no curve inward) and

clench the love muscle tightly. Hold for three seconds and release, letting the ankles move back out a little. Alternate pulling in and clenching with the butterfly. ×10

2. Kneeling bridge. Kneel and sit back on your heels. Put your hands palms down behind you and thrust your pelvis upward, arching your back as high as you can. Exhale and clench your muscle hard. Hold for a count of five, and relax. Inhale. ×5

3. Buttocks thigh stretch. Kneel and keep your back rigid down to the buttocks. Raise your arms out straight to chest level and rock back gripping with your buttocks. Rock as far back as possible each time, keeping the breasts taut and the buttocks clenched. Begin the pulse with each rock back. At the farthest leanback, clench hard. ×10

EXERCISE WHILE AEROBIC DANCING

1. Crossovers. With feet comfortably set apart, put your arms out to the sides, jump up and cross your right foot and right arm over the left. Clench your muscle, and jump back to start. Cross left arm and leg over right and jump, clench, and jump back to start. ×40

2. Lunges. From standing start lunge to the right, with right leg forward in a bent position, back leg straight. Alternate and swing your arms up high. With each lunge, clench your muscle as you go down on the leg. ×20. (Don't attempt lunges unless you are thoroughly warmed up.)

3. High kicks. Jump and kick your right leg bent, jump and kick your right straight. Jump and kick

your left leg bent, jump and kick your left leg straight. Repeat and clench at each kick. ×10 on each side.

4. Boxing. As you run in place and begin your arm exercises, start to clench each time you box out your arm. To the right, box and clench, and to the left, shoot that arm out, box and clench. ×30

5. Down and out. Stand in a straddle, arms to the side, and bend. Then, to the beat, push to the front, push ×10 and clench, then hit the floor with your hands and clap while bouncing ×10, and bending your knees ×10, reach between your legs as far back as you can and up. And again.

6. Jog for cooldown. Begin your two-minute cooldown jog and clench with each heel strike. Arms above head, and stretch.

Fitness Class

1. Pelvic raises. When you reach this point in your fitness class, combine your love muscle exercises with your routine. Arms at sides and knees bent, clench muscle and buttocks and raise the hips. Your weight is on your feet and shoulders. Push higher and clench. Stay there and pulse to the count of ten and release. ×5

2. Bridge. On your back, arms behind head, legs bent, lift up in an arched position like a bridge. Try to get your head off the floor and dangling. (Make certain your back is already well warmed up.) At the highest point clench hard and hold. ×3

3. Butterfly. Knees out in the butterfly, heels

together, and hands on your ankles. Alternate the butterfly × 10, trying to touch your knees to the floor on each side, with body bends over the legs. Then grasp ankles firmly, pull them in, and clench at the same time. Clench and hold to a count of three and release. × 10

4. Lower back straightener. Lie on the floor with your knees bent. Then very slowly, keeping your lower back in contact with the floor at all times, slide the legs out on the floor until you feel the back lifting off. Slide them all the way out and begin again. This is the best possible exercise for straightening and aligning the spine and the pelvis. Bend knees again and make sure spine is touching the floor, and as the knees begin to slide out, clench and release repeatedly. When the spine lifts off the floor, cease love muscle exercises. Repeat × 6

5. Tuck and sway. Kneel and go down on all fours. Lower your elbows until your head can be grasped in your hands. Then pull *gently* on your head, releasing the tension in the neck and shoulders. × 5. Sit up to inhale, and kneel again. Then round your back deeply like a cat, and as you tuck your buttocks under, clench hard. Release, and lift your neck up to the sky, arching your back down. Clench and release. Alternate your back up and down, clenching at each position. × 10

6. Rocking chair. Lie on your stomach, grasp your ankles in each hand, arch up your neck and shoulders, and pull on the ankles, hard. Force your thighs out against the resistance of your hands and make a reverse bridge, or rocking chair. Rock back and forth,

rolling on your stomach, and clench with each rock. Inhale and release. ×5

7. Stretching wide. With your legs spread as wide as possible, put your hands behind your buttocks and inch your buttocks forward while straightening your back. Push your hands together at breast level and hold the resistance in your arms for a count of five. Release, exhale, and again, clenching at the same time. Release, exhale, and bend as far forward as possible, arms out in front. Lie down if possible on the floor, keeping knees straight and toes pointed, and push. Clench, release, and alternate arms. Then swing to the right leg, swing to the center, swing to the left leg and up. ×5

Health Club/Weight Training

Women now do weight training for body shaping and toning, as a sport in itself, and as an adjunct to training in almost any kind of competition. If you work out at a health club, or are doing weight training, your warm-up routine can include any of the preceding warm-up exercises in running, aerobic dance, or fitness class. Add this one for some spectacular before-you-do-the-machines results.

Abdominal Stress. Lie on the floor and hold on to the leg of some nearby machine, making sure you have a clear space around your legs. Then, while keeping your spine firmly on the floor, put your legs together, and slowly lift and circle them around from the waist. Keep them just above the floor and go to waist height at the right, around to straight out, and as low to the floor as possible in front of you, and around and up to the left, keeping just above the floor, and raise them back to vertical. Begin again and work up to ten circles. Then reverse the direction of the circle. × 10 Each time your legs lower in front of you clench your love muscle and try to hold it for the full circle. Relax when your legs come up to vertical. Breathe.

On the Nautilis. During any arm exercises, such as pulling the weights forward to meet in front of your chest, clench as the effort is being made. That is, tighten as you take in air.

Leg Raises. If you use-the-leg-raise handles set in a frame, place your back into the frame and grasp the handles firmly. Now clench your stomach and love muscles firmly, and raise both legs simultaneously until they parallel the floor. Hold to a count of three and release. Make sure your back is firmly pressed against the floor. × 10

Five-pound weights. If you are using weights while on a bench, hold one five-pound weight firmly in both hands, with your knees on either side of the bench. Swing it in a controlled way above your head, keeping a firm grip on it. Do not go below the level of your head. Feel the stretch in your chest and the pack of your arms. Clench firmly as you hold and bounce the weight, and come back and over. × 10

Pull downs. As you kneel to pull the weights down behind your head and shoulders, clench with each pull down. Your coach or program planner can advise you on all repeats.

* * *

As you can see, there are many appropriate places to combine love muscle exercises throughout your weight-training routine.

Swimming

If you are doing laps, stretch before entering the pool by bending down and touching your toes at each side. Put your arms above your head and stretch them toward the ceiling. Repeat, and combine with clenching pattern. In the water, do one lap going up slowly with clenching every stroke, and one lap coming down fast(er) with no clenching.

If you are in competition or doing *competitive workouts*, combine love muscle exercises with warm-ups as described, and with your weight training. In the pool combine them with distance patterns, for example with ×8 or ×6 laps. They work well with a pyramid, and with one up slow, one down fast. Do not combine with anything less than two laps, but try this (practice only): clench before racing dive and hold for entire one-lap sprint (except fly).

All through your exercises, when your love muscle is working, it cannot help but demand more oxygen to work with. When you do your exercises standing up or sitting straight, you will notice an increased and natural wish to expand the chest and hold it higher, to give the lungs more room to expand. This brings in more oxygen and is very beneficial to your whole body.

More to Think About

Frequently in social situations, when people find out I am a sex therapist, the tone and content of the communication changes. Some people have questions about their personal sex lives. Others titter, become embarrassed, change the subject, or get angry. Many become visibly nervous, stop making eye contact, and start telling inappropriate jokes, usually sexual in content. Then there are the not-so-subtle invitations to give private sexual instruction. These diverse emotional reactions have convinced me more than ever that people crave sexual knowledge and yet still don't know how to talk about sex comfortably.

As Roger Libby points out, most of us lacked sex-positive role models to shape the way we learned about the birds and the bees. Well, now we do. My goal in writing this book was to dispel the misinformation and myths that still envelope sex and the study of sex.

It's clear that there is a strong connection between good health through exercise and good sex. I hope that the readers of this book will take sex education into their homes. After all, we are all human and sexual.

I also hope that the reader does not allow any stereotypic model of orgasm or ejaculation to control his or her personal sex life, or to create additional performance anxiety about sexual behavior. Keep in mind the nonmodel of orgasm. Each of us has an idiosyncratic pattern of experiencing and expressing orgasm. Enjoy that specialness; it's what makes you YOU!

Selected Bibliography

Barbach, Lonnie, *For Yourself: The Fulfillment of Female Sexuality*. New York: Doubleday, 1975.

Beauvoir, Simone de. *The Second Sex*. New York: Bantam Books, Inc., 1952.

The Boston Women's Health Book Collective. *Our Bodies Ourselves: A Book by and for Women*. New York: Simon & Schuster, 1973.

Brecher, Ruth and Edward. *An Analysis of Human Sexual Response*. New York: Signet, 1966.

Comfort, Alex, Ph.D. *The Joy of Sex: A Gourmet Guide to Lovemaking*. New York: Crown Publishers, Inc., 1972.

Cooper, Mildred and Kenneth. *Aerobics for Women*. New York: Bantam Books, 1981.

Deutsch, Ronald. *The Key to Feminine Response in Marriage*. New York: Ballantine Books, Random House. 1968.

Dodson, Betty. *Liberating Masturbation*. New York: Bodysex Designs, 1974.

Friday, Nancy. *Forbidding Flowers*. New York: Pocket Books, 1975.

Fixx, James. *The Complete Book of Running*. New York: Random House, 1977.

Graber, Ben, and Georgia Kline-Graber. *Women's Orgasm: A Guide to Sexual Satisfaction*. New York: Bobbs-Merrill, 1975.

Haeberle, Erwin. *The Sex Atlas*. New York: Seabury Press, 1978.

Hartman, William E., Ph.D., and Marilyn A. Fithian. *Treatment of Sexual Dysfunction*. Long Beach Center for Marital and Sexual Studies, 1972.

Heiman, Julia, et. al. *Becoming Orgasmic: A Sexual Growth Program for Women*. New York: Prentice-Hall, 1976.

Hite, Shere. *The Hite Report*. New York: Macmillan Publishing Co., 1976.

Kaplan, Helen Singer. *The New Sex Therapy*. New York: Brunner and Mazel, 1974.

Kegel, A.H. "Sexual Functions of the Pubococcygeus Muscle," *Western Journal of Surgery*, Vol. 60, No. 10 (1952), pp. 521–524.

Kinsey, Alfred C., et. al. *Sexual Behavior in the Human Female*. New York: Simon & Schuster, 1953.

Koedt, Ann. "The Myth of the Vaginal Orgasm," *Liberation Now*, ed. Deborah Babcox and Madeline Belkin. New York: Dell Publishing Co., 1971.

Lauersen, Neils and Steven Whitney. *It's Your Body: A Women's Guide to Gynecology*. New York: Playboy Press, 1980.

Levin, Robert J., et. al. *The Pleasure Bond*. New York: Bantam Books, 1976.

Lopicolo, Leslie and Joseph. *Handbook of Sex Therapy*. New York: Plenum Press, 1978.

Masters, William, and Virginia Johnson. *Human Sexual Response*. Boston: Little, Brown and Co., 1966.

Millman, Marcia. *Such a Pretty Face: Being Fat in America*. New York: W.W. Norton and Co, 1980.

Morrison, Eleanor S., and Mila Price. *Values in Sexuality: A New Approach to Sex Education*. New York: Hart Publishing, 1974.

Nass, Gilbert, et. al. *Sexual Choices: An Introduction to Human Sexuality*. Monterey, Cal.: Wadsworth, 1981.

Otto, Herbert and Roberta. *Total Sex*. New York: Signet, 1973.

Rosenberg, Jack Lee. *Total Orgasm*. New York: Signet, 1973.

Scully, Diana. *Men Who Control Women's Health*. Boston: Houghton Mifflin Co., 1980.

Sherfey, Mary Jance. *The Nature and Evolution of Female Sexuality*. New York: Random House, 1966.

Slinger, Penny, and Nix Douglas. *Sexual Secrets*. New York: Destiny Books, 1979.

Talese, Gay. *Thy Neighbor's Wife*. New York: Doubleday, 1980.

Washburn, Susan. *Partners: How to Have a Loving Relationship After Women's Liberation*. New York: Atheneum, 1981.

SIGNET Books of Special Interest

Buy them at your local

bookstore or use coupon

on next page for ordering.

SIGNET Books You'll Enjoy